AMERICAN
COUNTRY
NEEDLEPOINT

AMERICAN
COUNTRY
NEEDLEPOINT

JIM WILLIAMS

The Taunton Press

Cover photo: **John Ryman**

Taunton
BOOKS & VIDEOS

for fellow enthusiasts

First printing: 1997
Printed in the United States of America

A THREADS book

THREADS® is a trademark of The Taunton Press, Inc., registered in the U.S. Patent and Trademark Office.

The Taunton Press, 63 South Main Street, PO Box 5506, Newtown, CT 06470-5506

Library of Congress Cataloging-in-Publication Data

Williams, Jim, 1950-
    American country needlepoint / Jim Williams.
        p.   cm.
    "A Threads book" — T.p. verso.
    ISBN 1-56158-171-2
    1. Canvas embroidery — United States — Patterns.
    2. Decoration and ornament, Rustic — United States.
    I. Title.
TT778.C3W554   1997
746.44'2041 — dc21   96-51013
                                                CIP

To simple childhood memories,
memories that are stitched
into a magical multicolored tapestry
of treasured moments
that only strengthen with time.
Love and thanks to all my family.

ACKNOWLEDGMENTS

Many people deserve my gratitude for their help with this book. First and foremost, I must find some way to thank my grandparents and relatives for their part in instilling in me the many fond memories that inspired the work within these pages. I can only hope that those now passed have some way to know of their contributions.

Thanks, too, to my parents, Robert and Elizabeth, for their part. I'm sure that my dad would be proud, and I know that my mother is. I think of them both very fondly.

My wife, Lynn, deserves some type of special and loving award. For well over a year, she's been watching me stitch and chart and write with piles of projects in seemingly every corner. My daughter, too, is very special. I can only hope that someday she looks back on her childhood with as many fond memories as I do on mine.

I should also thank Mary Ann and Gordon Patrick, for without their yarn shop and continued guidance, encouragement, and friendship during my early stitching career, there would be no needlepoint for me today. Thanks, too, to the Patricks and to Jilann Severson for the use of the Zinnia and Southwestern Hen pillows from their collections.

My brother Tom, a designer and craftsman in his own right, adapted the twig frame for the Country Rose Wreath from the design of my dear friend Abby Ruoff's book *Making Twig Furniture and Household Things*.

Margaret Sindelar deserves a special tribute as well. A superb seamstress and technician, she assembled many of the professionally finished creations that you see here.

CONTENTS

INTRODUCTION

For as long as I can remember, I have always loved nature. Growing up in the 1950s in the small village of Fayetteville in central New York afforded me many opportunities to explore and experience the wonder of nature around me, and these early influences are reflected in my needlework today.

As a small child, I lived with my parents and maternal grandparents in a large house on the edge of the village with acreage and a rustic, rather dilapidated barn. My grandfather was a small-time farmer in his spare time—when I was very little he kept a cow. Later, it was a billy goat, with whom I shared a mutual dislike, and then followed a yardful of colorful, proud, strutting chickens. Dogs and cats were constants, and transient or injured animals both wild and tame came and went. And, of course, we had several gardens—corn, pumpkins, potatoes, a grove of pear trees, a strawberry patch, and my grandmother's much-loved flower beds of roses, peonies, poppies, and zinnias.

Many of my fondest memories revolve around the simple times I had as a child exploring, playing, and helping with "chores." I remember, at age four or five, helping Grandpa pick strawberries; loading the wooden quart box to the brim with fat, juicy berries, and then running off to give it to Mom. I remember, too, when I was older, many summers of delightful play—exploring the wilds of the gully in the back and making many expeditions to the uncharted territory of the creek down below.

There were summer evening swims in nearby Cazenovia Lake and lots of summer visits to my father's relatives' camp on Oneida Lake. Aunt Florence and Uncle Herm's summer place was another world of wonder for a 10-year-old Tom Sawyer: hiking on a winding trail to Sand Beach, boating off to the island across the bay for an adventure, and checking the progress of Uncle Herm's garden in the back lot with its pole beans, tomatoes, cabbages, rows of colorful, spiky gladioli, and grapevines that reached up into the pine trees at the edge of the woods.

Nature and art first melded earlier while, as a young child, I would sit at my great-grandmother's knee as she hand-painted china with delicate flowers. To keep an active tot busy, and to instill a love of arts and crafts, Grandma Larabee would provide me with a stack of paper plates, which I carefully decorated with bouquets of crayoned flowers. Later, as my interest in drawing and painting grew, I revisited my childhood haunts with pen and palette, painting the woods, ravines, and creek I knew so well and the animals and flowers I loved so dearly.

Art became my course of study, and eventually I went on to teach arts and crafts in a local high school. I became interested in needlepoint soon after I was married. My wife bought canvas and yarns for a chair seat, but quickly discovered that she really didn't enjoy doing the work. Always intrigued with textiles, and not wanting to waste the money spent on the materials, I finished the piece and discovered that needlepoint was quite restful and relaxing after a hectic day with 180 high school kids.

Having successfully completed one piece, I found that I could design pieces to stitch with my own subject matter. Quickly following were dining-chair seats with songbirds and fruit—cardinals in Uncle Herm's grapevines, blue jays in wild blackberry brambles, and orioles in elderberry at creek's edge.

Pillows and rugs soon flowed from my fingers, and always the flowers and animal friends from childhood seemed to reappear in countless stitches and intricate detail. I began to sell my needlework pieces in galleries and my original designs to magazines and books.

Needlepoint and crafts became an even more integral part of my life when we moved to the Midwest, and I became a crafts editor for Meredith Corporation. There, my crafts design, stitching, and photo-styling abilities blossomed, and soon I found myself working on crafts and Christmas decoration for *Better Homes and Gardens*. After several years of design and editorial work for the magazine, a move to

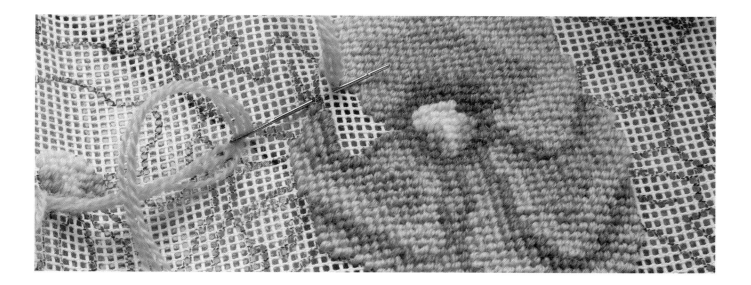

New York City and the prospects of freelance design opened up further possibilities for my unique approach to nature-inspired needlepoint and crafts design.

A Unique Approach to Needlepoint

Because of my art and design background, I suspect that I approach my work differently from most needlepoint designers. I don't spend long hours painting my subject on canvas with oil or acrylic and then stitching with matching wools. Nor do I chart the design prior to stitching. Instead, I draw a simple permanent-marker outline onto the canvas, tracing the original sketch from graph paper or newsprint. In some instances, I make a small sketch and then enlarge it by copy machine to the desired size before tracing it onto the canvas.

After selecting the predominant colors of yarns, I literally "paint" with the fibers to create the shading of my subject. Those of you who have an artistic side or a feeling for color,

light, and shade may wish to experiment with my technique on pieces of your own.

To begin, I sketch a few lines for shading onto the canvas outline. Usually, I'll break the area down into three areas—highlight, base color, and shadow—and select the appropriate yarn colors to match. Sometimes, however, I'll expand the colors with another two or three shades for a more realistic and subtle shading. Highlight and shadow are the first to be stitched, followed by thin, transitional areas of the additional shades that will work into the base color of the subject. To finish the area, I fill in the base color.

I'm always intrigued by the colors of yarns and the texture of various materials. To this end, I am not a traditional needlepointer, and I can hardly be called a purist. Rather, I view myself as something of a renegade in the needlepoint world. I don't work solely with traditional tapestry wools. I'm always on the lookout for materials or techniques that I can incorporate into my design that will give it an exciting and unexpected texture to imitate nature and provide a tactile feast for the senses.

In addition to the wonderful needlepoint wools available in a myriad of marvelous colors, knitting yarns of every persuasion are incorporated into my pieces. Whether knitting worsted wool, cottons, linens, or synthetic blends, any yarn can be called into service for interesting color and texture. All you need to make sure of is that the fibers are of equal weight (double or triple yarns if necessary) and that they can be threaded through your needle and the holes of the canvas. I have even been know to stitch with fine jute cording, twine, and common string for rustic, natural effects.

I'll admit that I don't follow the rules. Anything that can be threaded and worked through the canvas is a potential fiber. Another rule I ignore is that I don't work my ends into previous stitches or catch them into the first few stitches. I knot my ends, simply because it's faster and easier, and the ends are ultimately unseen. I'll let you decide whether you want to adopt my somewhat risqué techniques and practices or prefer to follow a more traditional approach to this centuries old form of stitching.

How to Use This Book

Each design in this book is an original subject inspired by my childhood memories of the simple, natural things around me, lovingly stitched and charted for you to duplicate. You'll find the "Country Animals" chapter alive with Grandpa's hens and roosters, a farm cat, baby bunnies in clover, a freshwater trout, and more. "Garden Fruits and Vegetables" is brimming with cabbage and caterpillar, Indian corn, Uncle Herm's Concord grapes, juicy watermelon, and quarts of berries. "Favorite Flowers" is blooming with brightly colored zinnias, blue hydrangeas, grandmother's fire-red poppy, and flower-garden rugs.

In addition to the clear, easy-to-read charts, you'll find sidebars throughout the book that teach you a new technique, stitch, or finishing detail. I've also included handy "quick-stitch tips"—short cuts to make your stitching easier and faster.

In perhaps the most innovative aspect of this book, I have incorporated other traditional American craft techniques with my needlepoint for truly unique and intriguing presentations. Trapunto, the art of sculpting by quilting and stuffing small areas, is combined with needlepoint to produce realistic robin's eggs in a nest and succulent strawberries in a quart basket. Traditional rug braiding with woolen cloth and crocheted rag rugs are used

to accent the finishing of pieces like the "Bird's Nest" cushion (see pp. 32-35) and the "Multiflower Bouquet Rug" (see pp. 92-97). Instructions for all the techniques are included to provide you with unlimited possibilities for creating your own needlepoint masterpieces.

The book concludes with a chapter on finishing, where you'll find detailed information on how to block your needlework piece, finish rugs, select fabric for pillows, and make your own piping, cording, and ruffles.

Whether you're a beginner, an intermediate stitcher, or an accomplished stitcher, there's something for you in *American Country Needlepoint.* There are small and quick-to-stitch designs that are only 6 in. square, standard pillows for a more involved project, and large-scale rugs for long-term stitching. And almost any of the designs can be adapted to suit your abilities.

If you're a beginning stitcher, you'll probably want to use full strands of Persian tapestry yarns and follow the chart closely. For the background, a

plain tent stitch or perhaps a fast and easy up-and-down long stitch might be best. But consider using different textures of wool, cotton knitting yarn, tweeds, or string to add interest.

If you're an intermediate stitcher, you may wish to try some of the textural stitches, experiment with blending yarns, or play with a variety of textured fibers. Let your creativity weave its way into your stitchery. If you're a more experienced stitcher, you can experiment freely with types and textures of yarns, try different stitches, and possibly custom-design the background to match your decor.

American Country Needlepoint is a very personal treasury of childhood memories and favorite things captured in stitches. It is my most sincere hope that some of the simple things and times I so dearly remember will touch you as well and kindle many warm memories. May you draw from those times and preserve them in your own loving stitches.

The yarn amounts given in the material lists in this book are based on 1½ yd. of Paternayan 3-ply Persian wool per sq. in. on #10 mono canvas. The amounts have been calculated as closely as possible, but they are approximates and should be considered as such. Purchase enough yarn of each color or dye lot to prevent shortages. Extra yarn may be returned or saved for your next project.

COUNTRY ANIMALS

From helping out
in my grandparents' chicken yard
to viewing prize-winning poultry
at the state fair,
I've always been fascinated by
the many colors and textures
of chickens' fabulous feathers.
Perhaps that's why these colorful birds
have made their way onto a
whole flock of my needlepoint pillows.
Start with this farmyard family,
and then turn your needle
to any and all of the
country animals that follow.

RED AND BLACK ROOSTER

Finished size: approximately 14 in. by 18 in.

A fine-feathered cock proudly displays his patterns of plumage to the delight of avid country stitchers. His colorful feathers are set off by a simple quick-stitch background and the addition of real tail feathers.

What You Need

- 14-in. by 18-in. piece of #10 mono natural canvas
- Tapestry needle
- Chicken tail feathers (available from millinery and fabric-trimming supply stores)
- Hot-glue gun and glue
- Yarns in the following colors and amounts (all colors are Paternayan 3-ply Persian wool unless otherwise noted):

For the head:

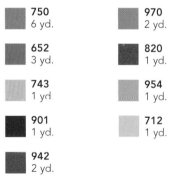

■	**750** 6 yd.	■	**970** 2 yd.
■	**652** 3 yd.	■	**820** 1 yd.
■	**743** 1 yd.	■	**954** 1 yd.
■	**901** 1 yd.	■	**712** 1 yd.
■	**942** 2 yd.		

For the background:

■	**752** 75 yd.

What to Do

To prepare the canvas for stitching, bind the raw edges with masking tape or fold over a ½-in. selvage to the back and machine-hem to prevent raveling.

To begin stitching, determine the placement of the pupil of the rooster's eye. To do this, turn to the chart on p. 11 and count the squares down from the top and in from the right side to the pupil. Mark the cross threads on the canvas with a fine-point permanent marker and work the stitch with three plies of 220 Black.

Following the chart, stitch the iris of the eye, and then continue to work the wattle, comb, and beak. If desired, make a small French knot (see the drawing at right on the facing page) using one ply of 261 White for an eye highlight.

For the body and tail:

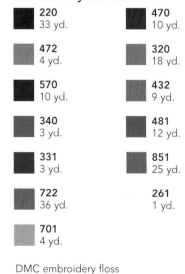

■	**220** 33 yd.	■	**470** 10 yd.
■	**472** 4 yd.	■	**320** 18 yd.
■	**570** 10 yd.	■	**432** 9 yd.
■	**340** 3 yd.	■	**481** 12 yd.
■	**331** 3 yd.	■	**851** 25 yd.
■	**722** 36 yd.	■	**261** 1 yd.
■	**701** 4 yd.		

DMC embroidery floss

■	**3826** 1 skein

Work the head with 851 Spice in tent stitch where indicated, and then continue with the neck in the scalloped-feather stitch described in the sidebar on the facing page.

Following the chart on pp. 10-11, work the breast and wing and continue on to complete the body and tail feathers.

When the rooster is complete, work the vertical ribbed background with 752 following the instructions in the quick-stitch tip on the facing page.

For the real feather accents, first block and assemble your pillow according to the instructions on pp. 99-103. Purchase feathers that curl in the direction of the needlepoint tail feathers. Study each feather to determine its best positioning. To attach each feather, trim the quill to about ¼ in. from the feather. Poke the quill into the needlepoint stitching at the desired location, add a drop of hot glue to the back of the feather, and press into place. Repeat for the other feathers, layering them atop the initial feathers in a natural manner.

Scalloped-Feather Stitch

This simple long stitch, or bargello pattern, creates an interesting texture that simulates the ordered arrangement of feathers. In addition, the scalloped-feather stitch is a great way to cover a large area quickly. For further interest, consider working the area with a different type of yarn: cotton, silk, bouclé, or even tweed.

Using three plies of Persian wool yarn or the material of your choosing, follow the stitching diagram below to work the scalloped feathers in rows. To prevent canvas distortion, alternate the rows as you stitch the area.

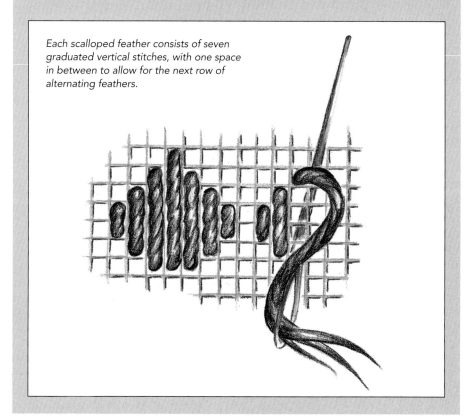

Each scalloped feather consists of seven graduated vertical stitches, with one space in between to allow for the next row of alternating feathers.

FRENCH-KNOT STITCH

To add a French knot, bring the yarn up through the stitching, wrap it around the needle, and then bring the needle back down through the stitching.

Quick-Stitch Tip:
Vertical Ribbed Background

The ribbed background of the rooster pillow is an easy and fast way to add textural interest to your needlepoint stitchery; it can be adapted to any number of subjects.

For best effect, choose a color of yarn that closely matches the natural shade of the needlepoint canvas. For the rooster, I chose 752, a mellow tan that complements the shade of the

#10 natural canvas. A similar effect could be achieved using white canvas and a white or an off-white yarn.

To work the background, stitch vertical rows across the canvas, skipping every other row. Leave these rows unstitched for the ribbed effect that suggests corduroy or corrugated cardboard.

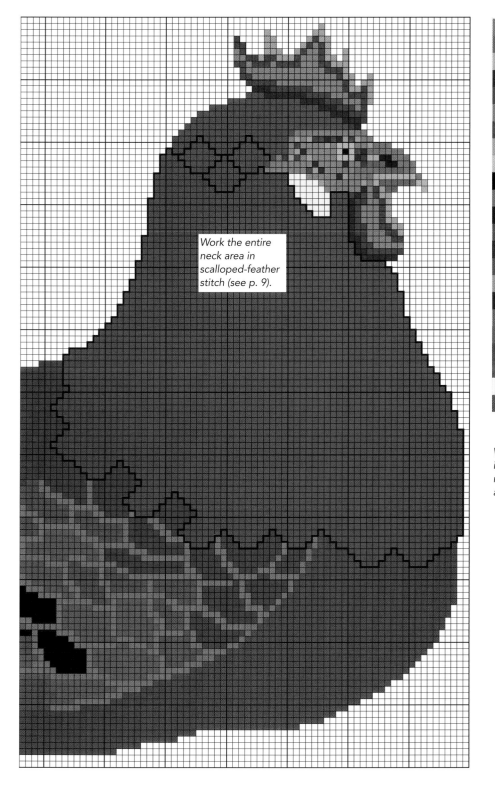

Work the entire neck area in scalloped-feather stitch (see p. 9).

750
652
743
901
942
970
820
954
712
220
472
570
340
331
722
701
470
320
432
481
851
261
3826 (DMC)

Work the background in alternating vertical rows of blank canvas and 752 wool.

BLACK SETTING HEN

Finished size: approximately 14 in. by 17 in.

*D*on't be fooled by the seemingly intricate texture and pattern of this plucky hen. I worked with a variety of different materials for effect, but even a novice can create a pillow to crow about with ordinary yarns and the basic tent stitch by following the quick-stitch tips presented here.

What You Need

- 18-in. by 22-in. piece of #10 mono canvas
- Tapestry needle
- Yarns in the following colors and amounts (all colors are Paternayan 3-ply Persian wool unless otherwise noted):

For the head:

950 1 yd.		945 1 yd.	
952 1 yd.		710 1 yd.	
943 1 yd.		237 1 yd.	
954 1 yd.			

For the eggs:

884 4 yd.		886 8 yd.	

For the background:

- Four different novelty yarns in natural shades totaling 216 yd. (see the sidebar on p. 14). If desired, use Paternayan alternatives 435, 444, 454, and 465.

What to Do

To prepare the canvas for stitching, bind the raw edges with masking tape or fold over a ½-in. selvage to the back and machine-hem to prevent raveling.

To begin stitching, determine the placement of the pupil of the hen's eye. To do this, turn to the chart on p. 14 and count the squares down from the top and in from the left side to the pupil. Mark the cross threads on the canvas with a fine-point permanent marker and work the stitch with three plies of 220 Black.

Following the chart, stitch the iris of the eye, and then continue to work the wattle, comb, and beak using all three plies of yarn. If desired, make a small

For the body:

220 54 yd.		260 12 yd.	
471 16 yd.		733 1 yd.	
222 27 yd.		671 1 yd.	
262 21 yd.		752 1 yd.	

DMC pearl cotton

318 1 skein	

Cresta d'Oro metallic yarn

Black Metallic 4 yd.	

Gray heather knitting worsted wool (or 200) 24 yd.	

Black-and-white tweed 21 yd. (or 1 strand of 220, 7 yd.; and 2 strands of 237, 14 yd.)	

French knot (see the drawing on p. 9) using one ply of 262 White for an eye highlight.

Work the head and neck with Cresta d'Oro Black Metallic, 220 Black, and 262 White, and then work the remainder of the body and the eggs following the chart. For stitching short cuts, see the quick-stitch tips below and on p. 15. Work the background following the instructions in the sidebar on p. 14.

Quick-Stitch Tip:
Dot Feather Pattern for Neck

Following the chart exactly to re-create the random dot pattern for the hen's neck can be confusing and time-consuming. To work this area more quickly, mark the outline of the neck onto your canvas with a fine-point permanent marker and then stitch the white dots in a random pattern across the area to simulate the original. Finish by filling in with black.

Simple Long-Stitch Background

For the background, select four coordinating natural novelty or knitting yarns for a textured effect, or use the alternative shades listed in the materials on p. 12.

   For the richly textured background of this pillow, I selected four very different yarns—a nubbly off-white cotton bouclé, a tan-and-white two-tone polyester, a tan worsted-weight synthetic, and a light brown worsted-weight synthetic. If you cannot find similar yarns, feel free to be creative with your selections—almost anything that can be threaded through the needle will work. Just be sure to keep a consistent yarn weight between the selections. Double finer yarns if necessary to equal those with more bulk.

   Cut each of the yarns into random workable lengths. Beginning in the upper-left-hand corner and working to the right, work the background in horizontal rows across the canvas using random selections of your background colors and following the stitching diagram below. To prevent canvas distortion, work the second row from right to left; alternate the remaining rows as you stitch the rest of the background.

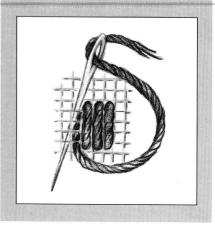

Quick-Stitch Tip:
Striped Feather Pattern for Back

To work the back easily, stitch all of the black (220) lines first and then fill in the remaining stitches with brown (471). For an even simpler time, mark the outline with a fine-point permanent marker following the chart and create your own free-form striped pattern.

Quick-Stitch Tip:
Tweed Texture for Rear

I chose a tweed knitting worsted-weight yarn for the rear of the hen. During stitching, the yarn frayed slightly and created nubbly bumps, which I found to my liking. If you feel uncomfortable with this approach, opt for a "tweed" of one strand of 220 Black and two strands of 237 Silver Gray.

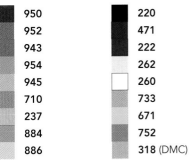

▮	950	▮	220
▮	952	▮	471
▮	943	▮	222
▮	954	▮	262
▮	945	▯	260
▮	710	▮	733
▮	237	▮	671
▮	884	▮	752
▮	886	▮	318 (DMC)

▮ **Black Metallic** (Cresta d'Oro)
▮ **Gray heather knitting worsted wool**
▮ **Black-and-white tweed**

BABY CHICK

Finished size: approximately 6 in. by 7 in.

*T*he newly hatched chick on this pillow was a birthday gift to my daughter. The baby chick makes a simple stitching project that really can be completed in just one day. The natural weave of the canvas provides a no-stitch background and a country flavor. What could be simpler?

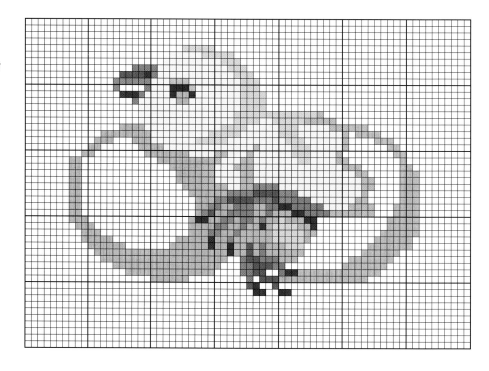

What You Need
- 9-in. by 10-in. piece of #12 mono natural canvas
- Tapestry needle
- Scrap of black fabric for backing canvas
- Yarns in the following colors and amounts (all colors are Paternayan 3-ply Persian wool unless otherwise noted):

For the chick:

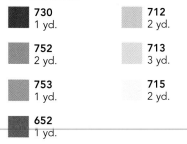

730 1 yd.	712 2 yd.
752 2 yd.	713 3 yd.
753 1 yd.	715 2 yd.
652 1 yd.	

DMC embroidery floss

744 1 skein	211 1 skein
519 1 skein	

For the egg:

455 3 yd.	263 2 yd.

What to Do
To prepare the canvas for stitching, bind the raw edges with masking tape or fold over a ½-in. selvage to the back and machine-hem to prevent raveling.

To begin stitching, determine the desired placement of the chick's eye on the canvas. Mark the cross threads of the canvas with a fine-point permanent marker and work the eye using six plies of the embroidery flosses 744, 519, and 211.

Using two plies of yarn, follow the chart to stitch the chick and the eggshells.

For quick stitching, leave the background blank. Back the canvas with a piece of black fabric when finishing. (For finishing details, see the finishing instructions and tips on pp. 99-103.) If you prefer a stitched background, select a background technique from any of the other projects in this book to give your baby chick a touch of your own personality.

SOUTHWESTERN HEN

Finished size: approximately 14 in. by 17 in.

The subtle whites of this plump country hen and the texture of the black-string, long-stitch background provide a striking graphic contrast that typifies many of the contrasting elements of southwestern landscapes and cultures. Scraps from a worn vintage Indian blanket and bead-wrapped cording make this piece truly a work of art.

What You Need

- 18-in. by 22-in. piece of #10 mono canvas
- Tapestry needle
- Yarns in the following colors and amounts (all colors are Paternayan 3-ply Persian wool unless otherwise noted):

For the head:

968	725
1 yd.	1 yd.
970	731
3 yd.	1 yd.
881	741
1 yd.	1 yd.
220	743
1 yd.	1 yd.

DMC embroidery floss

817	309
1 skein	1 skein

For the body:

212	246
2 yd.	10 yd.
445	260
30 yd.	144 yd.

DMC pearl cotton

Ecru
1 skein

For the background:

- 1 ball or cone of black string (available from weaving supply shops as cotton warp)

For bead finishing (if desired):

- Black-and-white seed beads
- Beading needle
- Quilting thread

What to Do

To prepare the canvas for stitching, bind the raw edges with masking tape or fold over a ½-in. selvage to the back and machine-hem to prevent raveling.

To begin stitching, determine the placement of the hen's pupil. To do this, turn to the chart on p. 20 and count the squares down from the top and in from the left side to the pupil. Mark the cross threads of the canvas with a fine-point permanent marker and work the stitch with three plies of 220 Black.

Following the chart, stitch the iris of the eye, and then continue to work the wattle, comb, and beak. If desired, make a small French knot (see the drawing on p. 9) using one ply of 260 White for an eye highlight.

Work the dot feather pattern (see the quick-stitch tip on p. 21) with 246 Neutral Gray, and then complete the body and tail feathers.

For the background, use two strands of black string and work the simple long-stitch background stitch described in the sidebar on p. 14.

Finish the pillow according to the instructions on pp. 99-103. For the beading details, follow the instructions in the sidebar at right.

see the chart on p. 20 • p. 21 • p. 9 • p. 14 • pp. 99-103

Bead-Wrap Technique

Thread the beading needle with a 24-in. to 28-in. length of quilting thread. From the back of the cording, put the needle through the cording near the needlepoint stitching and secure.

Thread about 18 to 20 beads, or as many as are needed, onto the thread and then push the needle up from the back of the cording next to the original needle entry, pulling the thread taut to wrap the beads around the cord. Continue for as many rows and with any combination of beads, as desired. To end, secure the thread at back of the cording; clip away any excess.

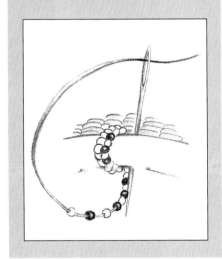

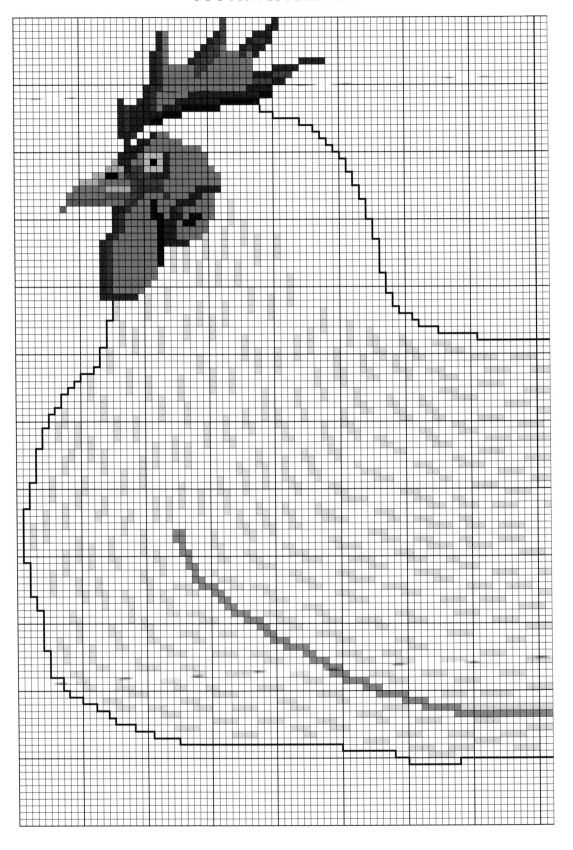

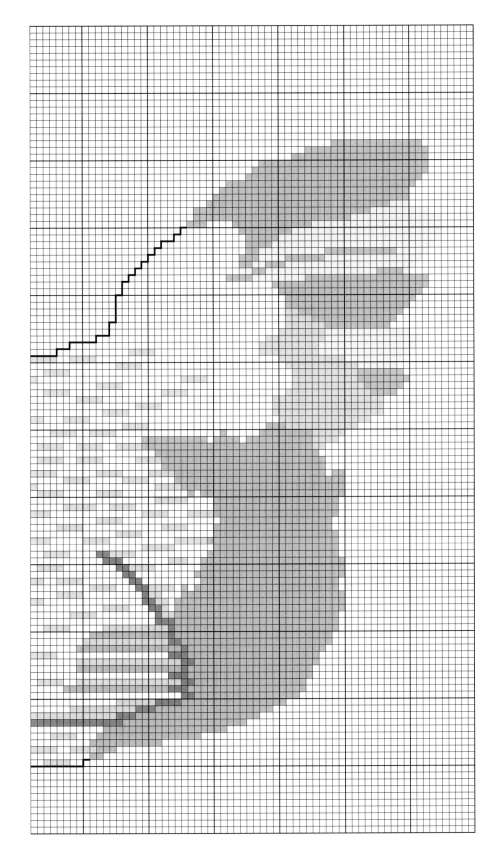

Quick Stitch Tip:
*Dot Feather Pattern
for Body*

Following the chart exactly to
re-create the random dot pattern
throughout the hen's body can be
confusing and time-consuming.
To work this area quickly, mark the
outline of the body onto your
canvas with a fine-point permanent
marker by following the chart.
Then, using the chart as only a
general guide for the areas with
dots, stitch random dots with
246 Neutral Gray to simulate the
original. Finish by filling in the body
by following the chart.

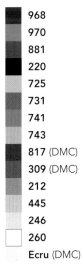

968
970
881
220
725
731
741
743
817 (DMC)
309 (DMC)
212
445
246
260
Ecru (DMC)

*Work the background using two
strands of black string.*

COCK CROWS AT DAWN RUG

Finished size: approximately 27 in. by 32 in.

*T*his crowing rooster stands proudly against a dawn landscape that forms the central panel of a striking rug that combines needlepoint and traditional rug braiding. His russet body and black tail plumes are accented with metallic threads and reflected in the shades of plaited wools that form the rug's border.

What You Need

- 18-in. by 24-in. piece of #10 mono canvas
- Tapestry needle
- Yarns in the following colors and amounts (all colors are Paternayan 3-ply Persian wool unless otherwise noted):

For the rooster:

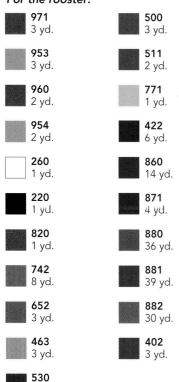

971 3 yd.	**500** 3 yd.
953 3 yd.	**511** 2 yd.
960 2 yd.	**771** 1 yd.
954 2 yd.	**422** 6 yd.
260 1 yd.	**860** 14 yd.
220 1 yd.	**871** 4 yd.
820 1 yd.	**880** 36 yd.
742 8 yd.	**881** 39 yd.
652 3 yd.	**882** 30 yd.
463 3 yd.	**402** 3 yd.
530 7 yd.	

DMC pearl cotton

823
1 skein

DMC embroidery floss

301 1 skein	**801** 1 skein
783 1 skein	**680** 1 skein
918 1 skein	

Cresta d'Oro metallic yarns
(or metallic threads of your choosing)

Bright Green 1 card	**Copper** 1 card
Dark Green 1 card	**Black** 1 card

For the background:

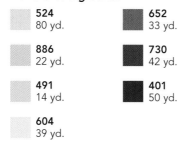

524 80 yd.	**652** 33 yd.
886 22 yd.	**730** 42 yd.
491 14 yd.	**401** 50 yd.
604 39 yd.	

For the braided border and finishing:

- Medium-weight wools—tweeds, herringbones, solids, etc.—in a variety of brown shades (about 4 yd. total)
- Carpet thread
- Sharp tapestry needle
- Fusible fleece or quilt batting to fit needlepoint
- Wool fabric to back needlepoint

What to Do

To prepare the canvas for stitching, bind the raw edges with masking tape or fold over a ½-in. selvage to the back and machine-hem to prevent raveling.

To begin stitching, determine the placement of the pupil of the rooster's eye. To do this, turn to the chart on p. 25 and count the squares down from the top and in from the right side to the pupil. Mark the cross threads of the canvas with a fine-point permanent marker and work the stitch with three plies of 220 Black.

Following the chart, stitch the iris of the eye, and then continue to work the wattle, comb, and beak. Work the body, tail, and legs.

For the background, work the landscape in stripes following the chart. Note that between each horizontal stripe on the chart there's a row of alternating stitches to help blend each color.

To assemble the rug, first block the needlepoint according to the directions on p. 99. Trim away the excess canvas, leaving a ½-in. selvage all around the stitching. Carefully clip the canvas at the corners.

Stitch a length of cording according to the instructions on p. 102, and then hand-stitch the cording to the needlepoint beginning at the bottom center of the stitchery. Fold the selvage to the back and blind-stitch the cording to the edge of the needlepoint.

Cut the wool into strips and braid as described in the sidebar on p. 24.

Braided Rug Technique

The outside edge of the "Cock Crows at Dawn" rug consists of 1-in.-wide braided wool coiled around the needlepoint center. To re-create this combination of techniques, cut the wools you've selected into 3-in.-wide strips. Roll up like-colored strips into balls and set aside.

To begin braiding, select two strips of different wools. (It's easiest to begin with two plaits of one color and one of another.) Fold in the raw edges of each strip, and then fold the strips in half lengthwise.

Place the raw end of one folded strip between the fold of the second strip, about one-third of the way into the strip (Step 1). To begin braiding, place the right-hand strip over the center (tucked-in) strip (Step 2). Next place the left strip over the former right (now center) strip (Step 3). Continue by bringing the tucked-in strip over the center to begin the 3-ply braid (Step 4). Work in this manner (Step 5) until the plait reaches about 6 ft. in length (or the desired length).

To add additional strips, trim the ends of the strips at a 45° angle. With the right sides together and aligning the points to the low ends of the angled strips, hand-sew the strips together with carpet thread.

To end the braid, trim about 6 in. to 8 in. off each strip at an angle so the strip narrows to about 1¾ in. wide. Continue braiding to the ends. Tuck under the raw ends and stitch to secure in place.

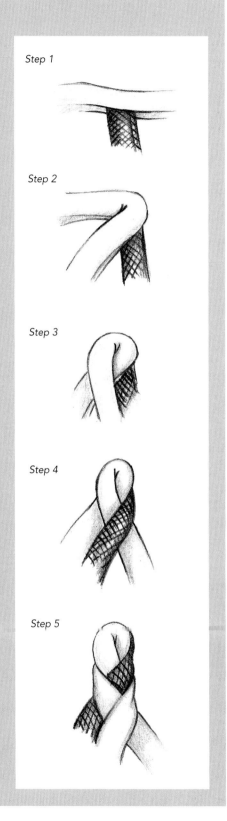

Step 1

Step 2

Step 3

Step 4

Step 5

Pad the back of the needlepoint with fusible fleece or quilt batting to make it the same thickness as the braid.

Beginning at the top left corner of the stitchery, fold the selvage to the back and blind-stitch the braid to the cording that surrounds the stitchery. Once around, sew the braid to the previously stitched coil. Continue until the entire braid is stitched in place; secure the end.

To finish the rug, cut a backing from the desired wool fabric using the needlepoint as a pattern. Add at least ½-in. selvage all around. Fold under the raw edges and hand-stitch the fabric to the edge of the first braided row to cover the batting.

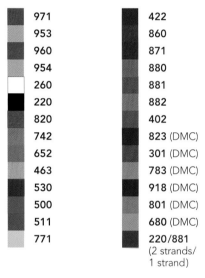

	971		422
	953		860
	960		871
	954		880
	260		881
	220		882
	820		402
	742		823 (DMC)
	652		301 (DMC)
	463		783 (DMC)
	530		918 (DMC)
	500		801 (DMC)
	511		680 (DMC)
	771		220/881 (2 strands/ 1 strand)

Bright Green (Cresta d'Oro)
Dark Green (Cresta d'Oro)
Copper (Cresta d'Oro)
Black (Cresta d'Oro)

Work the background in stripes following the numbers on the chart. For the second stripe from the top, use two strands of 524 and one strand of 886.

COCK CROWS
AT DAWN RUG

524

524/886

886

491

604

652

730

401

RABBITS IN CLOVER

Finished size: approximately 12 in. square

Early summers brought batches of baby bunnies hopping through the fields and clover patches. Stitch this adorable pair of rabbits using realistic tones, and then surround them with red clover and a tweed background.

What You Need

- 15-in. square of #10 mono canvas
- Tapestry needle
- Sharp-pointed tapestry needle
- Yarns in the following colors and amounts (all colors are Paternayan 3-ply Persian wool unless otherwise noted):

For the rabbits:

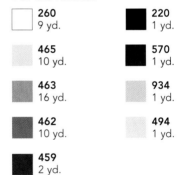

260 9 yd.		220 1 yd.	
465 10 yd.		570 1 yd.	
463 16 yd.		934 1 yd.	
462 10 yd.		494 1 yd.	
459 2 yd.			

What to Do

To prepare the canvas for stitching, bind the raw edges with masking tape or fold over a ½-in. selvage to the back and machine-hem to prevent raveling.

To begin stitching, center the design within the hemmed canvas (see the chart on p. 28). For best effect, work the rabbits first and then follow with the clover.

Finish the stitching by filling in the background using a worsted-weight tweed knitting yarn or, if you prefer, two plies of 412 Brown and one ply of 600 Forest Green Paternayan wool.

For the clover:

624 12 yd.		610 3 yd.	
632 8 yd.		350 10 yd.	
630 48 yd.			

DMC embroidery floss

3609 1 skein		917 1 skein	
3607 1 skein			

For the background:

412 80 yd.		600 40 yd.	

or 1 skein of brown/olive tweed knitting yarn (or color desired)

For the three-dimensional texture of the clover blossoms, use six plies of embroidery flosses 3609, 3607, and 917. Following the clover-stitch diagram below, work the clover petals over the needlepointed clover. To simulate the overlapping petals of the blossoms, stitch from the top down using the three shades of floss. Work the stitches on the blossoms near the rabbits, or on as many of the blossoms as desired.

LAZY-DAISY CLOVER STITCH

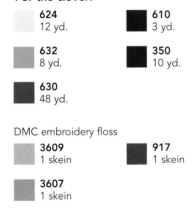

For each petal of the clover blossom, create a loop of floss and then secure to the needlepoint as indicated. Vary the shades for a three-dimensional effect.

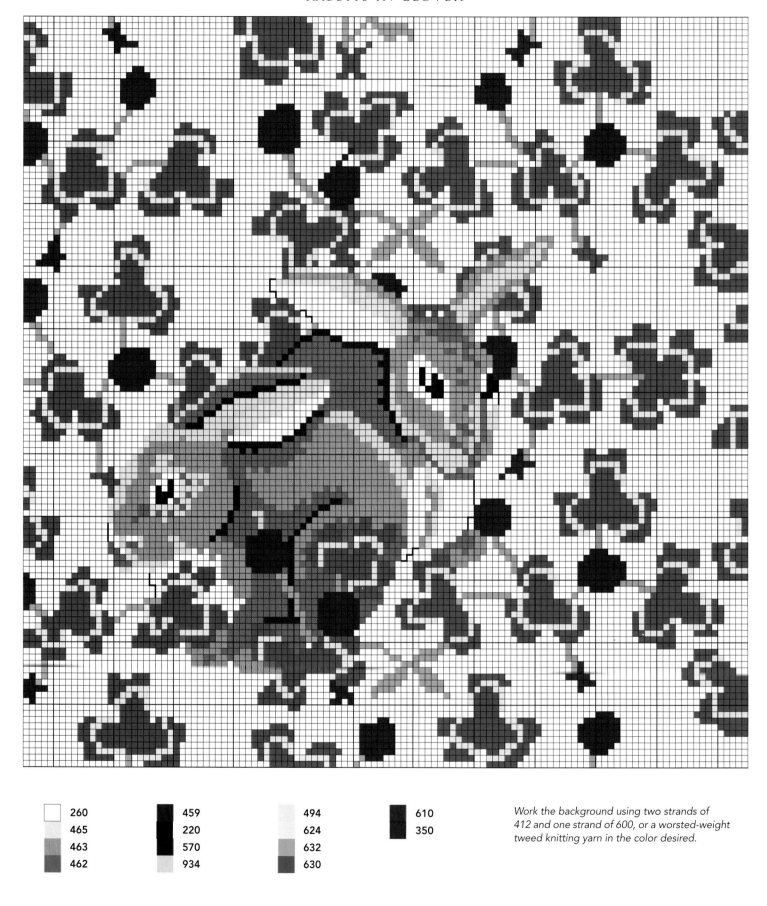

	260		459		494		610
	465		220		624		350
	463		570		632		
	462		934		630		

Work the background using two strands of 412 and one strand of 600, or a worsted-weight tweed knitting yarn in the color desired.

RAINBOW TROUT

Finished size: approximately 11 in. by 17 in.

Calmly floating in a shallow stream, this rainbow trout is sure to catch the eye of stitchers and anglers alike. For the submerged effect, the colors of the fish and plant are blended in rows with graduated shades of watery blue green.

What You Need

- 15-in. by 21-in. piece of #10 mono canvas
- Tapestry needle
- Yarns in the following colors and amounts (colors for the fish are DMC embroidery floss; all other colors are Paternayan 3-ply Persian wool):

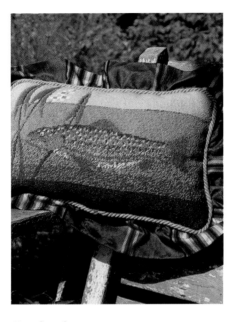

For the fish:

DMC embroidery floss

415 2 skeins		**341** 1 skein	
400 2 skeins		**598** 1 skein	
301 2 skeins		**945** 1 skein	
317 2 skeins		**3743** 2 skeins	
822 2 skeins		**3041** 1 skein	
760 2 skeins		**453** 1 skein	
3778 1 skein		**Snow White** 1 skein	

For the plant:

710 1 yd.		**651** 5 yd.	
756 2 yd.		**692** 12 yd.	
745 1 yd.		**690** 4 yd.	
652 5 yd.			

For the background:

578 60 yd.		**521** 32 yd.	
523 60 yd.		**423** 36 yd.	
522 12 yd.			

What to Do

To prepare the canvas for stitching, bind the raw edges with masking tape or fold over a ½-in. selvage to the back and machine-hem to prevent raveling.

To begin stitching, center the design within the hemmed canvas (see the chart on p. 30). For best effect, work the design in the horizontal stripes of the sky and various water levels. To achieve the underwater effect, all areas below the waterline (including the fish) are worked with blended stitches.

First, work the upper plant and sky area (A) using all three plies of wool. Next, work the single row (C) for the surface of the water.

Work the first water level (B) using two plies of 523 and one ply of 522. For the fish, use six plies of embroidery floss with one strand of 522.

Continue working the design in color stripes of water and stream bottom (C, D, and E) following the color key of the chart. For the fish, use six plies of embroidery floss with one strand of the appropriate shade for blending water.

RAINBOW TROUT

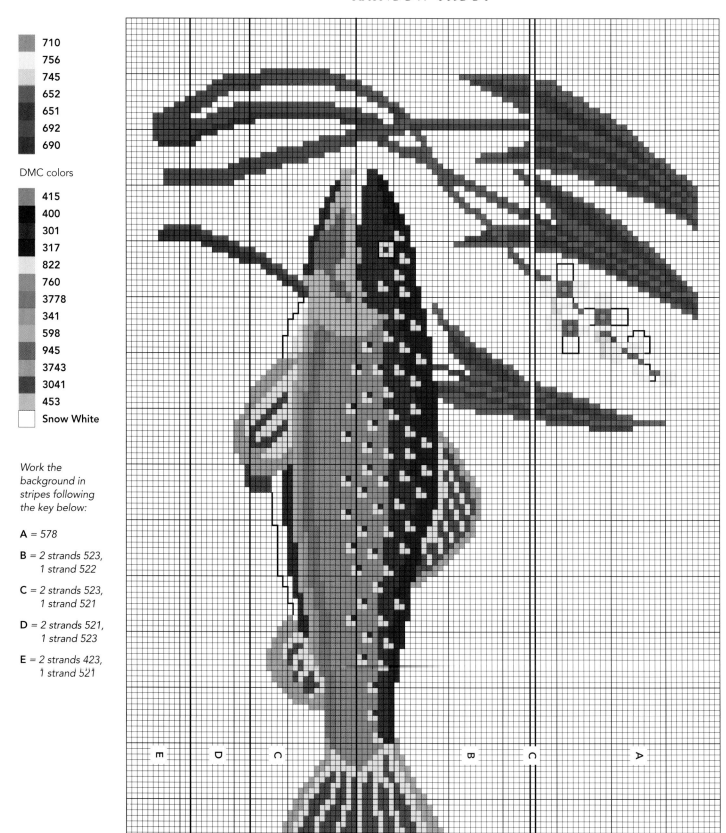

710
756
745
652
651
692
690

DMC colors

415
400
301
317
822
760
3778
341
598
945
3743
3041
453
Snow White

*Work the
background in
stripes following
the key below:*

A = *578*

B = *2 strands 523,
1 strand 522*

C = *2 strands 523,
1 strand 521*

D = *2 strands 521,
1 strand 523*

E = *2 strands 423,
1 strand 521*

BIRD'S NEST

Finished size: approximately 10 in. in diameter

A tiny nest with realistically shaded eggs forms a cushion that sports a unique combination of American craft techniques. Encircling a center of needle-point with three-dimensional trapunto eggs is a "nest" of coiled braided wool.

What You Need
- 8-in. square of #12 mono canvas
- Tapestry needle
- Yarns in the following colors and amounts (all colors are Paternayan 3-ply Persian wool):

For the eggs:

595 2 yd.	594 2 yd.
524 3 yd.	522 2 yd.

For the background:

450 5 yd.	470 5 yd.
495 5 yd.	750 4 yd.

For the trapunto technique:
- 6-in. square of cotton fabric
- Cotton balls or polyester fiberfill

For the braided nest:
- Medium-weight wools—tweeds, herringbones, solids, etc.—in a variety of brown shades (about 1 yd. total)
- Carpet thread
- Sharp tapestry needle

What to Do
To prepare the canvas for stitching, bind the raw edges with masking tape or fold over a ½-in. selvage to the back and machine-hem to prevent raveling.

Before stitching, create the sculptured trapunto eggs according to the sidebar below. Following the chart and using two plies of yarn, stitch the trapunto eggs first, and then fill in the background of the nest.

Quilted Trapunto Technique

To create the trapunto eggs, first place the canvas atop the full-scale pattern on p. 34 and trace over the eggs with an indelible marker.

Machine-stitch the cotton fabric to the back of the canvas atop the marker lines, leaving a ½-in. opening for stuffing. Trim away the excess fabric from the back to about ⅛ in. from the stitch line.

Stuff each egg with cotton balls or small amounts of fiberfill to the desired fullness (see the photo below) and hand-stitch the openings closed.

Stitch the eggs following the chart on p. 35.

The outside edge of the "Bird's Nest" cushion consists of ¾-in.-wide braided wool coiled around the needlepoint center. To re-create this combination of techniques, cut the wools you've selected into 2½-in.-wide strips. Roll up like-colored strips into balls and set aside.

To begin braiding, select two strips of different wools. (It's easiest to begin with two plaits of one color and one of another.) Fold in the raw edges of each strip, and then fold the strips in half lengthwise.

Place the raw end of one folded strip between the fold of the second strip, about one-third of the way into the strip (see the drawing in the sidebar on p. 24). To begin braiding, place the right-hand strip over the center (tucked-in) strip. Next place the left strip over the former right (now center) strip. Continue to braid in this manner until the plait reaches about 6 ft. in length (or the desired length).

To add additional strips, trim the ends of the strips at a 45° angle. With the right sides together and aligning the points to the low ends of the angled strips, hand-sew the strips together with carpet thread.

To end the braid, trim about 6 in. to 8 in. off each strip at an angle so the strip narrows to about 1¾ in. wide. Continue braiding to the ends. Tuck under the raw ends and stitch to secure in place.

To assemble the braided coil, first block the needlepoint according to the directions on p. 99. Trim away the excess canvas, leaving ½-in. selvage all around the stitching. Carefully clip the canvas every ½ in. all around.

Beginning at the bottom center of the stitchery, fold the selvage to the back and blind-stitch the braid to the edge of the needlepoint stitching. Once around, sew the braid to the previously stitched coil. Continue until the entire braid is stitched in place; secure the end.

To finish the cushion, cut a backing from the desired wool using the needlepoint and braiding as a pattern. Add at least ½-in. selvage all around.

Stitch a length of cording according to the instructions on p. 102, and then hand-stitch the cording to the braided circle. Clip the selvage of the backing and hand-sew it to the cording, leaving an opening for stuffing. Stuff lightly with polyester fiberfill and sew the opening closed.

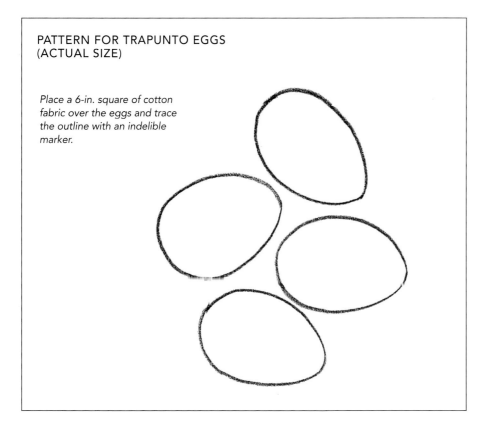

PATTERN FOR TRAPUNTO EGGS
(ACTUAL SIZE)

Place a 6-in. square of cotton fabric over the eggs and trace the outline with an indelible marker.

595
524
594
522

470
750
450/495
(1 strand each)

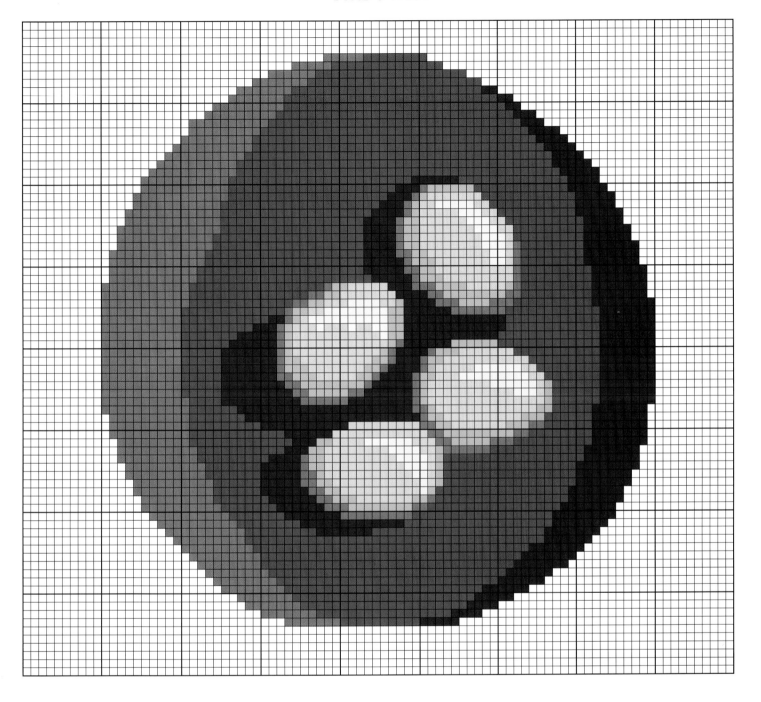

FARM CAT

Finished size: approximately 15 in. by 20 in.

I t seems that there were always cats around as I was growing up, and most of the time they were outside cats. First there was Tippy, then Molly and Joyce. George, pictured here, is a later buddy, but he captures the quintessential country farm cat curled up for a nap.

What You Need

- 18-in. by 24-in. piece of #10 mono canvas
- Tapestry needle
- Yarns in the following colors and amounts (all colors are Paternayan 3-ply Persian wool):

For the cat:

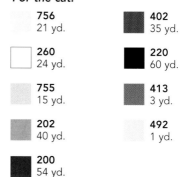

756	21 yd.	402	35 yd.
260	24 yd.	220	60 yd.
755	15 yd.	413	3 yd.
202	40 yd.	492	1 yd.
200	54 yd.		

For the background:

432
75 yd.

What to Do

To prepare the canvas for stitching, bind the raw edges with masking tape or fold over a ½-in. selvage to the back and machine-hem to prevent raveling.

To begin stitching, determine the placement of the pink of the cat's inner ear. To do this, turn to the chart on p. 38 and count the squares up from the bottom and in from the left to the start of the pink ear. Mark the cross threads of the canvas with a fine-point permanent marker and work the inner ear using 492 Flesh.

Continue to work the cat by following the chart, stitching the black stripes and then the white and shaded areas. Finish the cat by filling in the grays using two plies of 202 and one ply of 402 for the light areas and two plies of 200 and one ply of 402 for the dark areas for a variegated fur effect.

For the wood-grain background, work the grain pattern following the chart, using three plies of 432 and the wood-grain long-stitch drawing at right.

see the chart on p. 38

Quick-Stitch Tip:
Wood-Grain Background

You can duplicate the easy-to-stitch wood grain without the use of the chart if you prefer. To do so, simply divide your canvas background into four vertical stripes or "boards," and then work a variety of wood-grain patterns across each board. Use the chart as a guide or look to real wood patterns in furniture and floors for ideas.

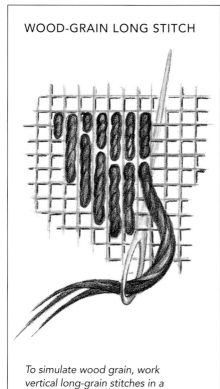

WOOD-GRAIN LONG STITCH

To simulate wood grain, work vertical long-grain stitches in a random angled pattern.

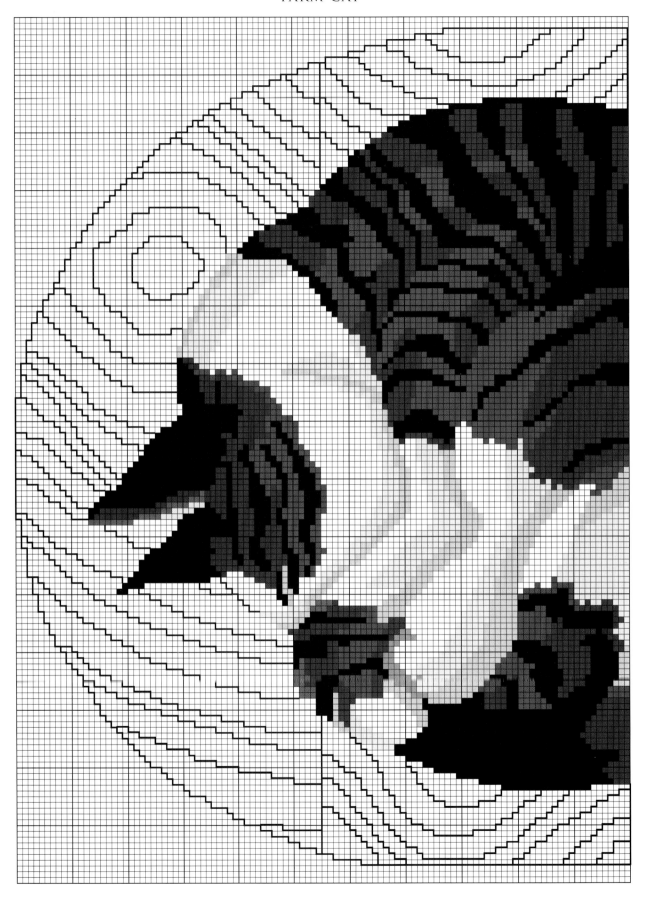

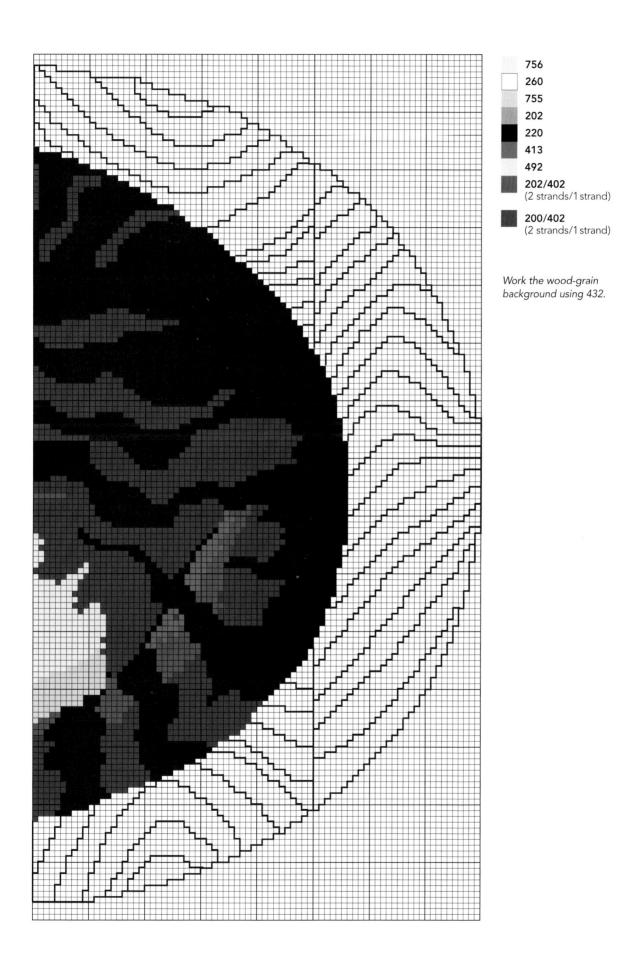

756
260
755
202
220
413
492
202/402
(2 strands/1 strand)
200/402
(2 strands/1 strand)

*Work the wood-grain
background using 432.*

GARDEN
FRUITS
AND
VEGETABLES

*Gardens are a staple of
country life and provide a bounty
of produce for the
summer table, as well as tasty
snacks stolen right off the vine.
Grandpa's watermelons,
grapevines, and berry patches were
forever being raided
for refreshing treats and are
just the beginning of a bushel of
country-fresh projects
for you to stitch.*

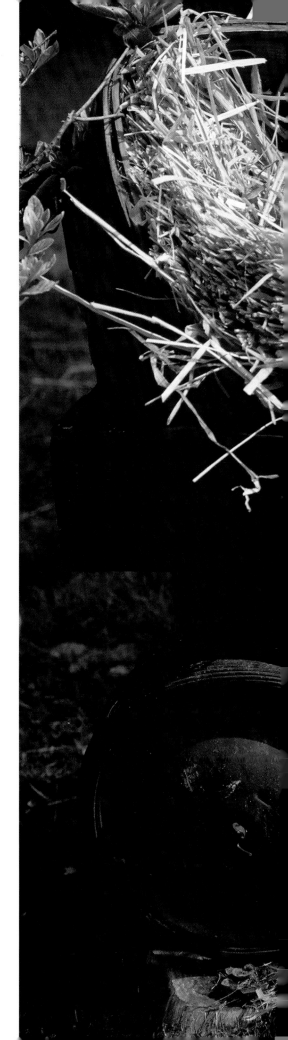

COUNTRY WATERMELON SLICE

Finished size: approximately 5 in. by 10 in. by 2 in.

This three-dimensional piece of watermelon is a slice of American folk art that will add an amusing and refreshing accent to your decor. Work the sculptured piece in four simple sections combining standard tent stitch with dainty petitpoint seeds, if desired, and then assemble by hand.

What You Need

- ½ yd. of #10 Penelope canvas
- Tapestry needle
- Yarns in the following colors and amounts (all colors are Paternayan 3-ply Persian wool):

For the rind:

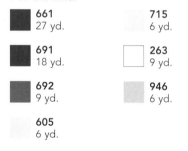

661 27 yd.	**715** 6 yd.
691 18 yd.	**263** 9 yd.
692 9 yd.	**946** 6 yd.
605 6 yd.	

For the fruit:

944 27 yd.	**942** 30 yd.
943 22 yd.	

For the seeds:

459 3 yd.	**263** (see above)

For finishing:

- Sharp tapestry needle
- Quilting thread
- 6-in. by 10-in. piece of 1½-in.-thick foam rubber

What to Do

To prepare the canvas for stitching, bind the raw edges with masking tape or fold over a ½-in. selvage to the back and machine-hem to prevent raveling.

For portability and ease of stitching, you may wish to cut the canvas into pieces for each section of the watermelon. To do this, determine the size of the finished stitchings and add at least 2 in. all around to each piece. Cut the pieces from the canvas and finish as described above.

To begin stitching, center the design within the hemmed canvas piece. Following the chart on the facing page, stitch each of the pieces, making sure to stitch two of the half-circle pieces for the front and back of the pillow.

Stitch the outer rinds first, and then work the remaining shades in toward the fruit. Work the stitches for the seeds prior to stitching the pinks of the fruit. If desired, stitch the seeds in petitpoint following the instructions in the sidebar at right. For stitching shortcuts, see the quick-stitch tip on the facing page.

Watermelon Assembly

To assemble the watermelon, block the pieces as necessary following the instructions on p. 99. Trim excess canvas to ½ in. all around.

With a sharp tapestry needle and quilting or heavy-duty thread, blind-stitch the outer rind to the curved portion of one of the half-circle pieces, clipping curves. If necessary, add stitching at the end with 661 to make the rind fit the curve.

Stitch the straight watermelon piece (the thickness) to the straight edge of the half circle, adding stitching to the rind with 661 if necessary. Stitch the ends of the piece to the ends of the outer rind.

With a marker, mark the foam to size and cut using a serrated knife. Insert the foam into the needlepoint pieces and blind-stitch the second half-circle piece in place.

Petitpoint and Penelope Canvas

Petitpoint is a fine needlepoint stitch that is a miniature version of the standard tent stitch. To work a section in petitpoint, you'll need to use Penelope canvas, a needle-point canvas that has double rows of threads woven both horizontally and vertically.

To stitch the petitpoint, use one ply of wool and a fine tapestry needle. Using the point of the needle, divide the double threads of the canvas in the desired area into a single-thread grid and stitch in tent stitch over the divided threads. For regular-sized stitching on Penelope canvas, work with three plies of yarn over the double threads.

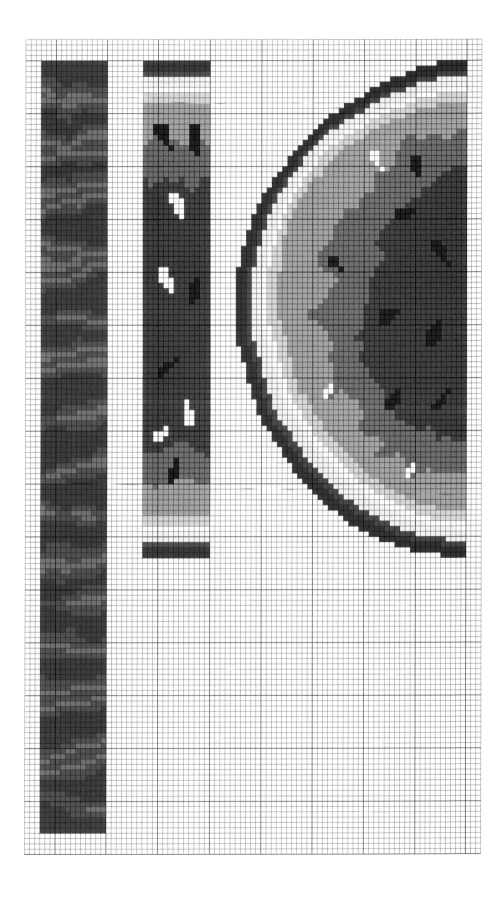

Quick-Stitch Tip

Even a novice stitcher can create a piece similar to this watermelon slice without needing to follow the chart. Using an indelible fabric marker, mark the perimeters of the sides and half-circle pieces onto the canvas and hem as described on the facing page. Sketch any seeds as desired onto the appropriate pieces, and work in either petitpoint or regular tent stitch using 263 or 459.

Following the colors indicated on the chart, stitch the rind colors from the outside toward the center in single rows. Fill in the remaining fruit with shades of pink working from lightest to darkest at the center. For the outer rind, stitch random stripes of 692 using the chart as a guide, and then edge with 691. Fill in the remainder with 661.

BERRY BASKETS

Finished size: approximately 3½ in. by 5 in. by 5 in.

J uicy, red strawberries from grandpa's berry patch and blackberries from the wild brambles made tasty treats all through the summer months. For a touch of summer all year long, stitch these sculptural needlepoint accents. The unusual trapunto quilting and beading techniques add to their realism, while natural raw silk suggests the wood grain of old-time quart baskets.

STRAWBERRY BASKET

What You Need

- 9-in. square of #12 mono canvas
- Tapestry needle
- 6-in. square of cotton fabric for trapunto backing
- Fabric marking pen
- Yarns in the following colors and amounts (all colors are Paternayan 3-ply wool unless otherwise noted):

For the berries:

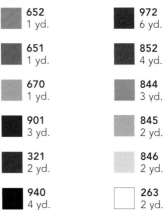

652 1 yd.	**972** 6 yd.
651 1 yd.	**852** 4 yd.
670 1 yd.	**844** 3 yd.
901 3 yd.	**845** 2 yd.
321 2 yd.	**846** 2 yd.
940 4 yd.	**263** 2 yd.

For finishing:

- Cotton balls or polyester fiberfill
- 3½-in. by 5-in. by 5-in. piece of foam rubber
- ¼ yd. raw silk for basket
- Matching thread
- 1-in. by 20-in. piece of lightweight cardboard for rim
- Flexible silver wire for staples
- Wire cutters
- Hot-glue gun and glue

What to Do

To prepare the canvas for stitching, bind the raw edges with masking tape or fold over a ½-in. selvage to the back and machine-hem to prevent raveling.

Before stitching, create the sculptured trapunto berries according to the sidebar at right.

Following the chart on p. 46 and working with two plies of yarn or six plies of embroidery floss, stitch the trapunto berries first. For best effect,

For the seeds:
DMC embroidery floss

434 1 skein	**973** 1 skein

For the basket:

151 6 yd.	**403** 1 yd.
442 6 yd.	

work along the stitch lines toward the center of the berries where possible. Next, work the flat berries.

Finish by stitching the perimeter of the square with the berry-basket colors.

Assemble the basket according to the instructions below.

Berry-Basket Assembly

To assemble, block the finished piece as necessary according to the instructions on p. 99. Trim the excess canvas to ½ in. all around.

From the raw silk, cut four 4½-in. by 6-in. pieces for the sides, making sure to align the grain along the short length of the sides. To shape the pieces

Quilted Trapunto Technique

To create the trapunto strawberries, first place the canvas atop the chart on p. 46 and trace over the five outlined berries with an indelible fabric marker.

Machine-stitch the cotton fabric to the back of the canvas atop the marker lines, leaving a ½-in. opening on each berry for stuffing (for reference, see the photo on p. 32). Trim away the excess fabric from the back to about ⅛-in. from the stitch line.

Stuff each berry with cotton balls or small amounts of fiberfill to the desired fullness and hand-stitch the openings closed.

Stitch the berries following the chart on p. 46.

STRAWBERRY BASKET

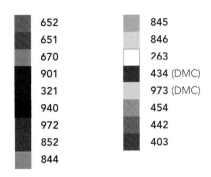

■ 652		■ 845	
■ 651		■ 846	
■ 670		□ 263	
■ 901		■ 434 (DMC)	
■ 321		■ 973 (DMC)	
■ 940		■ 454	
■ 972		■ 442	
■ 852		■ 403	
■ 844			

Bold lines on the strawberry-basket chart at right denote raised (trapunto) berries.

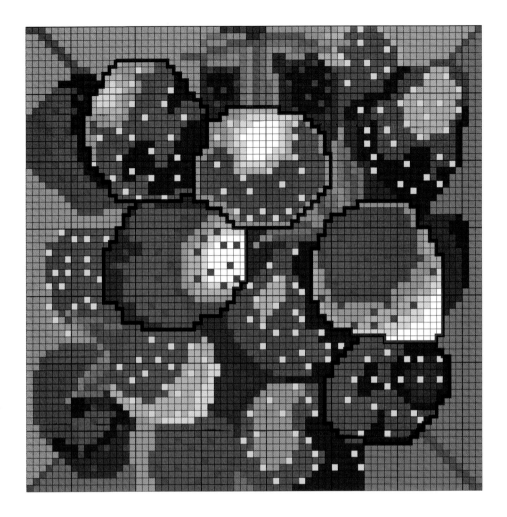

like a basket's sides, mark ½ in. in on both sides of one 6-in. side of each piece with a fabric marker. This will be the bottom edge of each basket side. From these points draw a line on each side to the top corners and cut, making a 4½-in. by 6-in. by 5-in. trapezoid for each side.

Cut one 5-in. square for the basket's bottom and one 1½-in. by 21-in. strip along the fabric's grain for the rim.

With right sides together, machine-stitch the top of each side to the edge of the needlepoint stitching with a ½-in. seam allowance. Pin the slanted sides of each side piece together and stitch with ½-in. seams. Clip away the excess fabric at the corners and turn to create the four sides and top of the berry basket.

Cut the foam rubber into a berry-basket shape by slanting the sides with a serrated knife. Insert the foam into the fabric basket. Fold in the raw edges and hand-sew the bottom piece to the sides.

To finish, cut a 1-in. by 20-in. strip of lightweight cardboard. Center the strip

atop the silk strip and, folding over the raw edges, glue the edges to the strip.

Starting in the center of one side, align the strip along the top edge of the berry basket. Fold the strip at each corner as you bend it around. Determine the placement of the wire "staples," two staples to a side, with fabric-pen dots about ¼ in. apart.

Cut eight 1-in. pieces of wire. To insert the wire, pierce the strip at each dot with a needle and then thread the wire through, twisting it in back to secure. Clip away any excess and bend the twisted portion down. Hot-glue the strip around the basket top for the rim.

BLACKBERRY BASKET

What You Need

- 9-in. square of #10 mono canvas
- Tapestry needle
- Fine tapestry needle for beading
- ⅛-in.-diameter glass rocaille beads in red, black, purple
- ⅛-in.-diameter iridescent red and iridescent purple iris rocaille beads
- Yarns in the following colors and amounts (all colors are Paternayan 3-ply wool unless otherwise noted):

For the basket:

■ 454 3 yd.	■ 403 1 yd.
■ 442 3 yd.	

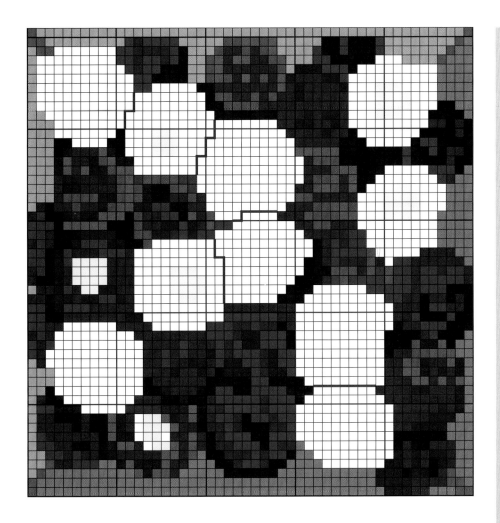

Work the white areas on the blackberry-basket chart above with beads and one ply of 220.

For the berries:

605
2 yd.

DMC pearl cotton

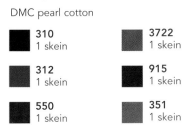

■	**310** 1 skein	■	**3722** 1 skein
■	**312** 1 skein	■	**915** 1 skein
■	**550** 1 skein	■	**351** 1 skein
■	**816** 1 skein		

For the beaded berries:

■ **220**
3 yd.

For finishing:
• The finishing materials are the same as those listed for the strawberry basket on p. 44 (minus the cotton balls or polyester fiberfill).

What to Do

To prepare the canvas for stitching, bind the raw edges with masking tape or fold over a ½-in. selvage to the back and machine-hem to prevent raveling.

To begin stitching, center the design within the hemmed canvas piece. Following the chart above, stitch the berries and all the berry centers, and then work the basket areas around the edge of the design. Finish by adding the beaded berries to the piece following the sidebar at right.

Assemble the piece according to the Berry-Basket Assembly instructions on pp. 44-46.

Glass-Beading Technique

Victorian needlepoint was often enhanced with the addition of beaded areas within the design. It's easy to adapt this technique to a country piece such as the Blackberry Basket shown here.

Each beaded area is comprised of the same simple tent stitch used throughout the stitchery, using just one ply of wool and a fine needle that is able to fit through the hole of each bead.

To work a beaded berry, bring the one ply of wool up from the back, thread on a bead in the desired color, and complete the tent stitch to secure the bead. Repeat for a second bead and additional beads until the canvas area of the berry is filled. For best effect and a realistic variety, work some berries with black, purple, and iridescent beads for riper berries, and some with purples and reds for those less ripe.

CABBAGE AND CATERPILLAR

Finished size: approximately 15 in. by 15 in.

Uncle Herm's vegetable garden on Oneida Lake in midsummer teemed with life, both his rapidly maturing plants and the colonies of garden insects that tried to steal their nourishment from them. Stitch Herm's robust, leafy cabbage, where a fat caterpillar quietly wriggles its way to its next meal.

What You Need

- 18-in. square of #10 mono canvas
- Tapestry needle
- ¼-in.-diameter yellow bead for cater-pillar head
- Yarns in the following colors and amounts (all colors are Paternayan 3-ply Persian wool unless otherwise noted):

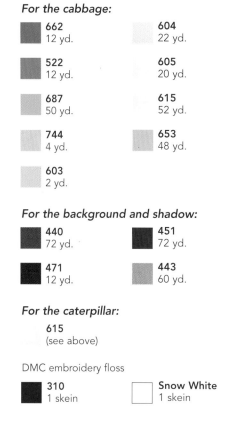

For the cabbage:

662 12 yd.		**604** 22 yd.	
522 12 yd.		**605** 20 yd.	
687 50 yd.		**615** 52 yd.	
744 4 yd.		**653** 48 yd.	
603 2 yd.			

For the background and shadow:

440 72 yd.		**451** 72 yd.	
471 12 yd.		**443** 60 yd.	

For the caterpillar:

615
(see above)

DMC embroidery floss

310 1 skein		**Snow White** 1 skein	

What to Do

To prepare the canvas for stitching, bind the raw edges with masking tape or fold over a ½-in. selvage to the back and machine-hem to prevent raveling.

To begin stitching, center the design within the hemmed canvas piece. Following the chart on p. 50, stitch the dark outlines of the cabbage leaves first to define the image. Next, work the veins of the leaves, and then the green areas in 687. Finish the cabbage by filling in the more subtle shades of the cabbage leaves.

To complete the stitching, work the shadow and finally the "dirt" back-ground using the tweed yarn tech-nique described in the sidebar on p. 50.

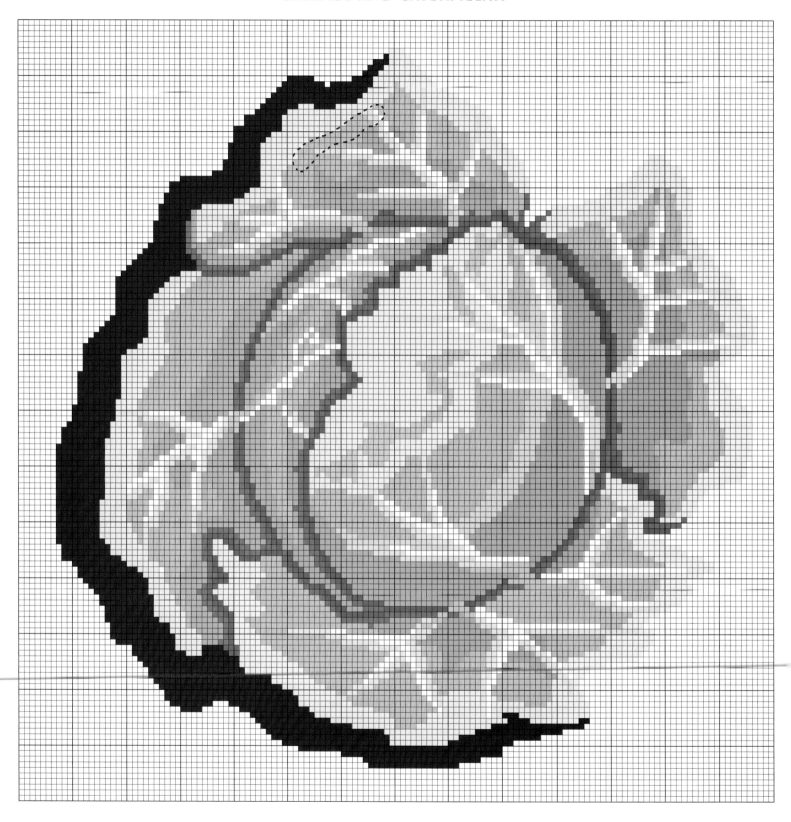

For the caterpillar, use two 3-ply strands of 615 with a large tapestry needle. Knot the yarn and bring it up through the finished stitching at one end of the caterpillar where indicated on the chart or at the desired location.

Tightly twist the yarn into a single coil, and then bring it back down through the stitching to the back for the body. Knot securely and trim away any excess.

Sew the bead to the front of the caterpillar for the head. Using six plies of floss, couch the twisted yarn body with black (310) and then white floss to create body stripes. Finish by adding antennae with two plies of black floss at both sides of the head.

	662			604
	522			605
	687			615
	744			653
	603			440/471/451 (1 strand each)

The dashed lines on the chart indicate the outline of the caterpillar.

Work the background with one strand each of 440, 443, and 451.

STITCHING THE CATERPILLAR

1. *Bring two 3-ply lengths of yarn up through the stitching.*

2. *Twist the lengths together tightly to make the body.*

3. *Bring the ends back down through the stitching and secure.*

4. *Add a bead for the head and couch with two plies of black floss for stripes.*

Textural Tweed Effect

Any background can gain textural interest with the use of a "tweed" yarn. To create this effect, simply use one strand each of three different colors. For the "dirt" in the cabbage pillow, I used one strand each of 440, 451, and 443. For the shadow, replace 443 with 471.

CONCORD GRAPES

Finished size: approximately 10 in. by 15 in.

I remember well the sweet fragrance and frosty purple-blue color of the grapes on my grandfather's prized arbors. In fall, heavy bunches hung amongst green, translucent leaves just waiting to be picked. Pick yourself a bunch or two with this pillow featuring grapes in those favored frosty colors.

What You Need

- 15-in. by 20-in. piece of #10 mono canvas
- Tapestry needle
- Yarns in the following colors and amounts (all colors are Paternayan 3-ply Persian wool):

For the grapes:

▪	**310** 12 yd.	▪	**342** 15 yd.
▪	**570** 10 yd.	▪	**343** 15 yd.
▪	**311** 22 yd.		

For the leaves:

▪	**691** 18 yd.	▪	**631** 25 yd.
▪	**692** 70 yd.	▪	**632** 22 yd.
▪	**662** 45 yd.		

For the vines:

▪	**482** 8 yd.	▪	**480** 8 yd.

For the background:

▪	**604** 45 yd.	▪	**615** 45 yd.

Vertical-Stripe Background

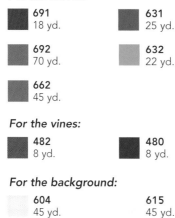

For a quick-to-stitch background with an interesting visual texture, work the area in alternating rows of two colors. For ease in stitching, work all of one color first, and then fill in the remaining rows with the second color.

It's easy to give any needlework this extra touch, and the effect can vary greatly with the choice of colors. For a subtle, textural background, as in the Concord Grapes pillow, choose two closely related shades like 604 and 615. For a more dramatic, bolder effect, opt for two stronger, contrasting shades. For best results, relate whatever colors you choose to the colors of the stitched image of your needlework.

What to Do

To prepare the canvas for stitching, bind the raw edges with masking tape or fold over a ½-in. selvage to the back and machine-hem to prevent raveling.

To begin stitching, center the design within the hemmed canvas piece. Following the chart on p. 54, stitch the grapes, leaves, and vines. Finish by working the background according to the instructions in the sidebar above.

CONCORD GRAPES

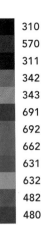

- 310
- 570
- 311
- 342
- 343
- 691
- 692
- 662
- 631
- 632
- 482
- 480

*Work the
background
in alternating
vertical rows of
604 and 615.*

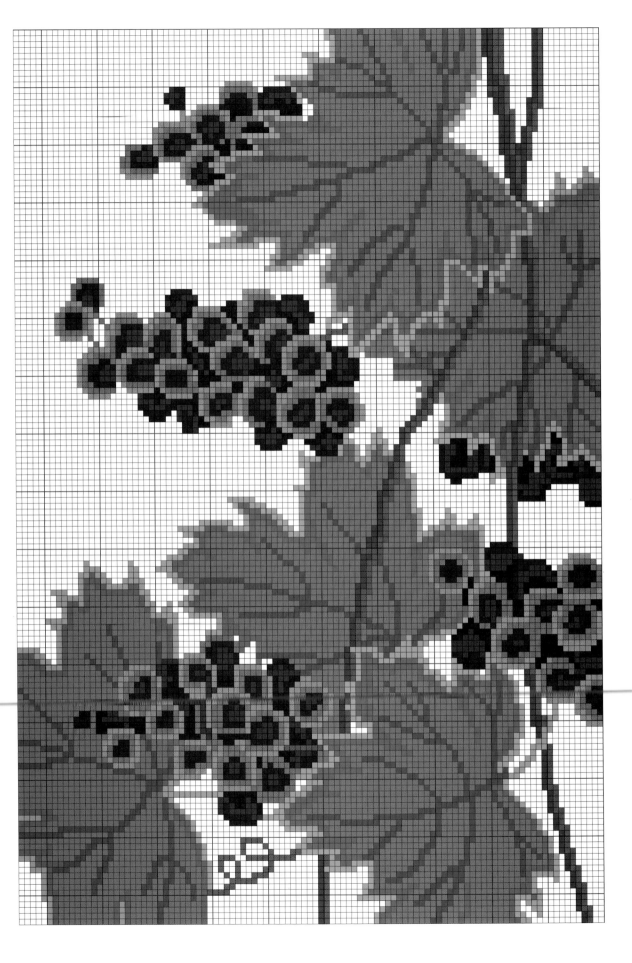

INDIAN CORN

Finished size: approximately 7 in. by 14 in.

The subtle colors and textures of Indian corn make it an intriguing and challenging subject for needlepoint. Try your hand at these colorful ears with a combination of Persian wools and shiny pearl cottons, then add three-dimensional tassels in a variety of materials for extra fun.

What You Need

- 12-in. by 18-in. piece of #10 mono canvas
- Tapestry needle
- Yarns in the following colors and amounts (all colors are Paternayan 3-ply Persian wool unless otherwise noted):

For the husks:

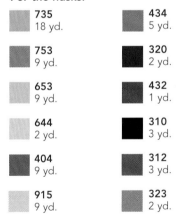

735 — 18 yd.	434 — 5 yd.
753 — 9 yd.	320 — 2 yd.
653 — 9 yd.	432 — 1 yd.
644 — 2 yd.	310 — 3 yd.
404 — 9 yd.	312 — 3 yd.
915 — 9 yd.	323 — 2 yd.

For the background:

260 — 49 yd.	514 — 12 yd.
553 — 26 yd.	512 — 12 yd.

What to Do

To prepare the canvas for stitching, bind the raw edges with masking tape or fold over a 1/2-in. selvage to the back and machine-hem to prevent raveling.

To begin stitching, center the design within the hemmed canvas piece. Following the chart on p. 56, stitch the husks first to define the ears of corn. Next work the kernels using pearl cotton.

To complete the stitching, work the gingham-check background following the sidebar on p. 56.

For the tassels, cut the desired materials into 3-in. or 4-in. lengths. Knot one end, and then sew each piece of yarn or floss up through the back of

For the kernels:

DMC pearl cotton

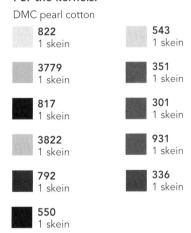

822 — 1 skein	543 — 1 skein
3779 — 1 skein	351 — 1 skein
817 — 1 skein	301 — 1 skein
3822 — 1 skein	931 — 1 skein
792 — 1 skein	336 — 1 skein
550 — 1 skein	

For the tassels:

- Assorted wool, embroidery floss, and string in varying shades of brown

the stitchery and through the brown tent-stitch ends of the ears. Continue until you have achieved the desired fullness. Trim the ends as needed to shape the tassels.

Quick-Stitch Tip

If desired, you can easily reproduce the look of these Indian corn kernels without having to follow the chart.

After completing the corn husks, simply divide the area of the kernels into a grid with a fine-point indelible fabric marker. Each section of the grid represents one kernel. For greater realism, do not line the squares up exactly, and make them smaller at the end of the corn. Then, group the colors for each ear together and begin stitching in a free-form manner. For best effect, work two or three of the colors as spots, and then fill in the kernels with the desired shades.

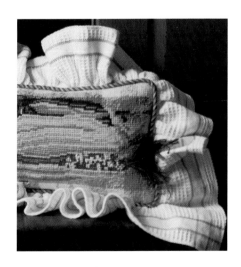

INDIAN CORN

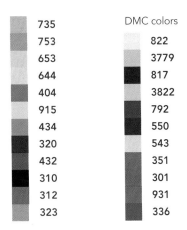

		DMC colors	
	735		822
	753		3779
	653		817
	644		3822
	404		792
	915		550
	434		543
	320		351
	432		301
	310		931
	312		336
	323		

Gingham Background

It's easy to give a country touch to your needlework with a striking faux-gingham background. The Indian Corn pillow is worked with a 1-in. square gingham, but you can vary the size of the check simply by working the squares in two-stitch or five-stitch squares, or any size you desire.

For the 1-in. gingham of this pillow, beginning in the upper-left corner and following the chart, work 10-stitch squares in 260 white across the canvas (#1 on the chart), and then work 553 blue as indicated (#4).

For the remaining squares to resemble the weave of gingham fabric, work the appropriate squares (#2) with two plies of 260 and one ply of 553, and (#3) with two plies of 553 and one ply of 260.

For the shadows of the corn on the gingham, repeat the process using the appropriate colors indicated on the chart:

    #5 = 514

    #6 = two plies 514, one ply 512

    #7 = two plies 512, one ply 514

    #8 = 512

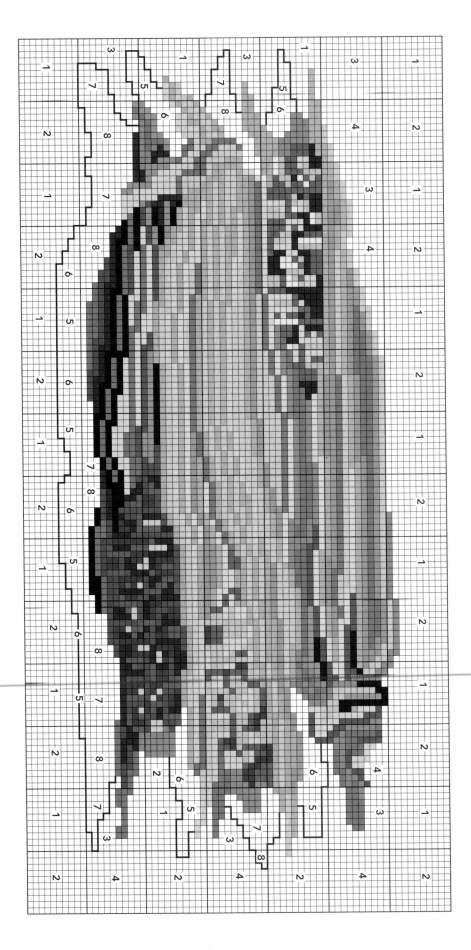

FAVORITE
FLOWERS

Ever since I was a youngster,
I have always had a passion for flowers.
I suppose that part of my interest
comes from the many shapes
and colors of nature that can be
found growing together—the
red-orange of oriental poppies,
the blue-violet of lush, round hydrangeas,
and the brightly hued petals
of the zinnia patch. Capture the colors
of these favorites for yourself,
and then select some of the
garden-inspired delights that follow.

PATCHWORK POPPY

Finished pillow size: approximately 12 in. square

A single fire-red poppy blooms against a natural-canvas background. For a quick, yet eye-catching project, stitch the needlepoint bloom as the focal point, and then add a pieced border in fabrics that accent its brilliant hues.

What You Need

- 10-in. square of #12 mono natural canvas
- Tapestry needle
- Yarns in the following colors and amounts (all colors are Paternayan 3-ply Persian wool unless otherwise noted):

For the petals:

■	970 12 yd.	■	930 8 yd.
■	952 14 yd.	■	900 4 yd.
■	843 5 yd.	■	541 6 yd.
■	880 6 yd.	■	311 2 yd.

For the center:

■	604 1 yd.		605 2 yd.

DMC pearl cotton

■ 823
1 skein

For the patchwork and finishing:

- Four 4½-in. by 7-in. pieces of red and pink checked linen, or desired fabric
- Four 4½-in. squares of natural linen for corner squares
- Matching threads
- ¾ yd. of black linen for backing canvas, pillow, and ruffle
- ½ yd. contrasting fabric for cording
- Purchased braided cording for around canvas
- Fusible fleece

What to Do

To prepare the canvas for stitching, bind the raw edges with masking tape or fold over a ½-in. selvage to the back and machine-hem to prevent raveling.

To begin stitching, determine the placement of the design on the canvas. Working with two plies of yarn, stitch the gray-green center following the chart on the facing page. Next, stitch the blue-black center with one strand of pearl cotton.

Continue the flower by stitching the blues and the dark outlines of the petals. Finish by filling in with the red and orange shades.

For quick stitching, leave the background blank. Back the canvas with a piece of black fabric when finishing. For the pieced patchwork, follow the instructions in the sidebar on the facing page.

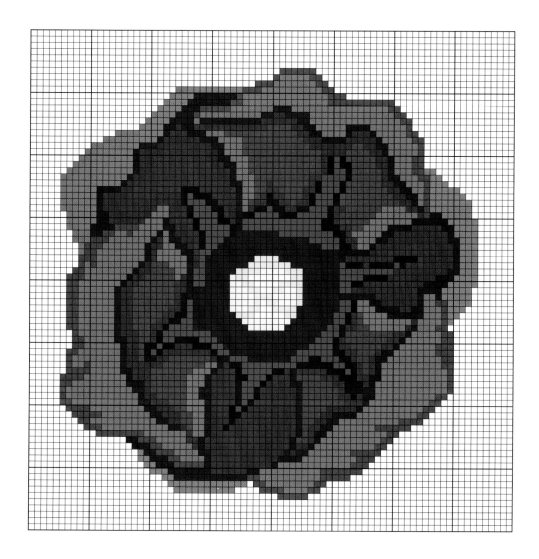

Quilted-Patchwork Assembly

It's easy to give your needlepoint a special look by combining it with the art of quilted patchwork. A patchwork border such as on the Patchwork Poppy pillow accentuates the stitching and is a fast way to make a larger piece from a tiny stitchery.

Begin by blocking the canvas according to the instructions on p. 99. Trim the canvas to the desired size, leaving a ½-in. selvage all around. Mark the square on the canvas with a pencil or a fine-point permanent marker to serve

as a guide. Cut a piece of black fabric to fit the canvas. Pin and machine-stitch the purchased cording to the canvas and black fabric.

With right sides together, sew two checked pieces to either side of the needlepoint poppy (for reference, see the photo on pp. 58-59). Press and set aside.

With right sides together, sew two linen squares to each short side of the remaining checked pieces. Press the seams open.

To assemble, sew one three-piece portion to the top of the poppy section, with right sides facing. Repeat for the bottom section, and press.

Cut the fleece to fit the pieced pillow front; pin in place and machine-topstitch ¼-in. from the seams with matching threads. Assemble the pillow according to the finishing instructions on p. 103.

ZINNIAS

Finished size: approximately 14 in. in diameter

A kaleidoscope of color in this vibrant bouquet recalls for me the hues in grandma's zinnia patch. Arranged in a circle of related shades, its many colors seem like a challenging project for flower-loving stitchers. But it's really just an allover pattern of petals—little areas of color to pick at one at a time.

What You Need

- 18-in. square of #12 mono canvas
- Tapestry needle
- Yarns in the following colors and amounts (all colors are Paternayan 3-ply Persian wool unless otherwise noted):

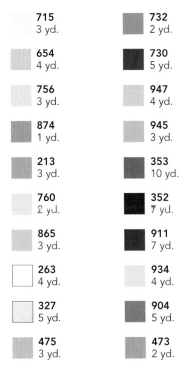

715 3 yd.	**732** 2 yd.
654 4 yd.	**730** 5 yd.
756 3 yd.	**947** 4 yd.
874 1 yd.	**945** 3 yd.
213 3 yd.	**353** 10 yd.
760 2 yd.	**352** 7 yd.
865 3 yd.	**911** 7 yd.
263 4 yd.	**934** 4 yd.
327 5 yd.	**904** 5 yd.
475 3 yd.	**473** 2 yd.

What to Do

To prepare the canvas for stitching, bind the raw edges with masking tape or fold over a ½-in. selvage to the back and machine-hem to prevent raveling.

When working with as many colors as are in the Zinnia pillow, it's essential to organize your materials. Before stitching, separate the yarns according to color families. Label each color with its color number as it appears on the key of the color chart on p. 64. This will facilitate your stitching and prevent you from misplacing yarns or using the wrong color.

To begin stitching, determine the placement of the design on the canvas. The design is primarily an allover pattern of petals that can easily be worked individually across the canvas. Using 2 plies of wool, 1 ply of pearl

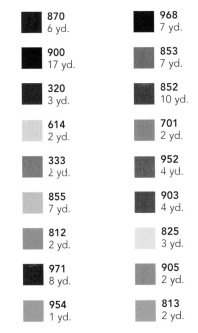

870 6 yd.	**968** 7 yd.
900 17 yd.	**853** 7 yd.
320 3 yd.	**852** 10 yd.
614 2 yd.	**701** 2 yd.
333 2 yd.	**952** 4 yd.
855 7 yd.	**903** 4 yd.
812 2 yd.	**825** 3 yd.
971 8 yd.	**905** 2 yd.
954 1 yd.	**813** 2 yd.

cotton, or 12 plies of embroidery floss, select a starting point to begin stitching. Some may wish to work a particular flower, like the white zinnia, first; others may wish simply to start at the upper-right-hand arc of the circle and stitch their way across.

Work the design across the canvas petal by petal, filling in the centers as you work as they are represented on the chart. For those centers left blank, use the long-stitch flower-center stitch shown in the drawing on p. 64, working with the brown center shades of your choosing.

For the three-dimensional and textural effects of the flower centers, personalize your work by using yarns of your choosing and the stitching diagrams on p. 65 to create the various textural stitches.

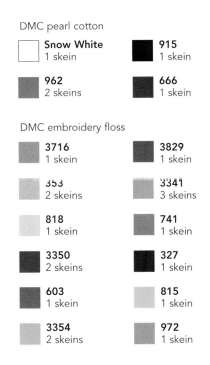

DMC pearl cotton

Snow White 1 skein	**915** 1 skein
962 2 skeins	**666** 1 skein

DMC embroidery floss

3716 1 skein	**3829** 1 skein
353 2 skeins	**3341** 3 skeins
818 1 skein	**741** 1 skein
3350 2 skeins	**327** 1 skein
603 1 skein	**815** 1 skein
3354 2 skeins	**972** 1 skein

ZINNIAS

715		968	
654		853	
756		852	
874		701	
213		952	
760		903	
865		825	
263		905	
327		813	
475		812/614	
732		(1 strand each)	
730			
947		DMC colors	
945		Snow White	
353		962	
352		915	
911		666	
934		3716	
904		353	
473		818	
870		3350	
900		603	
320		3354	
614		3829	
333		3341	
855		741	
812		327	
971		815	
954		972	

LONG-STITCH FLOWER CENTER

A simple long stitch worked in a circle creates a textured flower center.

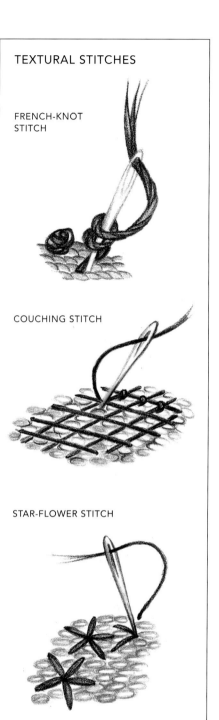

FRENCH-KNOT
STITCH

COUCHING STITCH

STAR-FLOWER STITCH

Use these decorative stitches atop the tent-stitched centers or on the canvas around the centers to add finishing details.

HYDRANGEA

Finished size: approximately 12 in. in diameter

Hydrangea blue is perhaps my favorite color in the summer garden, although there is really no one such shade at all. Hydrangeas come in an endless variety of tints that constantly tease me to duplicate them in wool on canvas. This single bloom features several of those elusive shades captured nosegay-fashion in a circle of fresh, green leaves.

What You Need

- 15-in. square of #10 mono canvas
- Tapestry needle
- Yarns in the following colors and amounts (all colors are Paternayan 3-ply Persian wool):

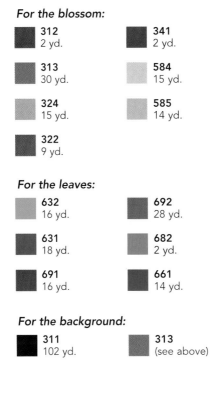

For the blossom:

312
2 yd.

341
2 yd.

313
30 yd.

584
15 yd.

324
15 yd.

585
14 yd.

322
9 yd.

For the leaves:

632
16 yd.

692
28 yd.

631
18 yd.

682
2 yd.

691
16 yd.

661
14 yd.

For the background:

311
102 yd.

313
(see above)

What to Do

To prepare the canvas for stitching, bind the raw edges with masking tape or fold over a ½-in. selvage to the back and machine-hem to prevent raveling.

To begin stitching, determine the placement of the design on the canvas. Working with all three plies of yarn, work the dark-green shadow with 661 to define the blossom area.

Beginning at the right side of the hydrangea, work the flower petal by petal, filling in the centers as you go.

When the flower is complete, work the veins of the leaves with 691. Next, work the outer edge of each leaf with 632 and 631. Complete the leaves by filling in the remaining areas, and then fill in the darker and smaller leaves at the right of the design.

Finish the pillow by working the pin-dot pattern with 313 following the chart on p. 68 and then filling in the background with 311.

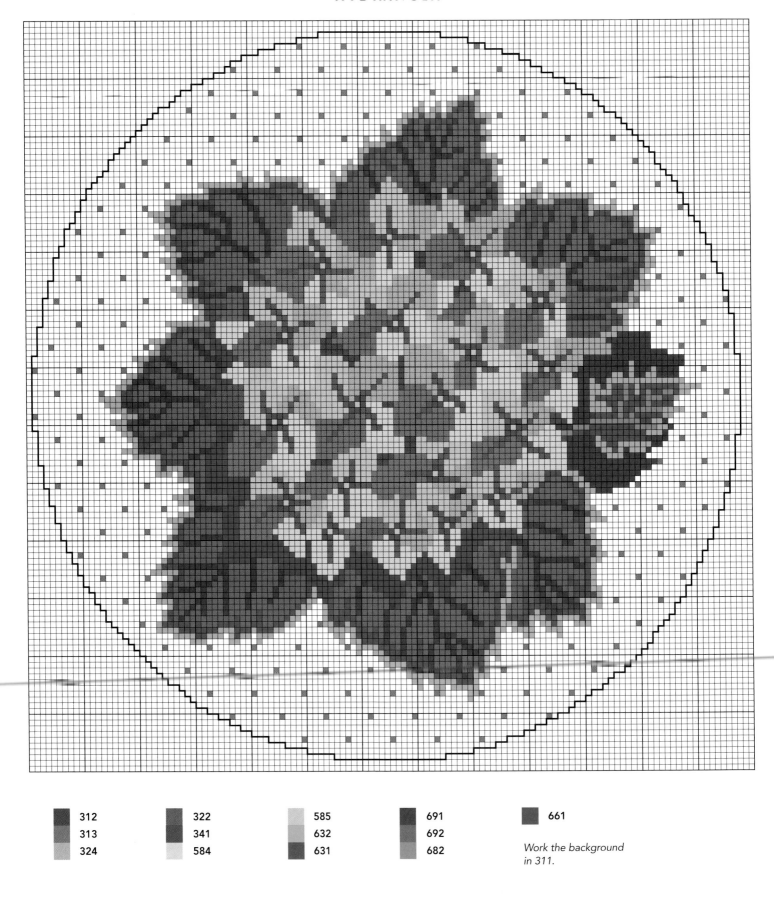

	312		322		585		691		661
	313		341		632		692		
	324		584		631		682		

Work the background in 311.

ALPHABET GARDEN RUG

Finished size: approximately 37 in. by 55 in.

A is for aster, B is for bluebell, C is for cyclamen. You can stitch a whole garden alphabet in a rug that will freshen your floor in true country style. Within a simple black grid, the alphabet and flowers alternate with squares of grab-bag scraps of multicolored stitching that recall vintage rag rugs and '40s linoleum flooring—a great way to use up leftover yarns!

What You Need

- 60-in. length of #10 mono canvas
- Tapestry needle
- Yarns in the following colors and amounts (all colors are Paternayan 3-ply Persian wool unless otherwise noted):

For the letters:

 **940**
182 yd.

For the grid:

 220
486 yd.

For the border:

710
280 yd.

For the letter backgrounds:

463
240 yd.

652
336 yd.

494
384 yd.

202
288 yd.

For the alternating background squares:

1,512 yd. of randomly cut mixed colors

For the flowers:

260 12 yd.	**861** 3 yd.	**693** 7 yd.	**652** 7 yd.
712 10 yd.	**940** 2 yd.	**672** 2 yd.	**820** 2 yd.
771 7 yd.	**431** 3 yd.		
710 5 yd.	**642** 8 yd.		
935 5 yd.	**671** 25 yd.		
947 6 yd.	**670** 10 yd.		
945 5 yd.	**632** 78 yd.		
943 4 yd.	**523** 30 yd.		
810 7 yd.	**522** 7 yd.		
972 4 yd.	**630** 60 yd.		
300 7 yd.	**610** 27 yd.		
330 6 yd.	**948** 3 yd.		
340 10 yd.	**653** 27 yd.		
344 6 yd.	**650** 8 yd.		
256 6 yd.	**673** 7 yd.		
521 3 yd.	**613** 3 yd.		
343 3 yd.	**812** 3 yd.		
584 2 yd.	**604** 6 yd.		
583 2 yd.	**694** 5 yd.		
581 2 yd.	**695** 4 yd.		

What to Do

To prepare the canvas for stitching, bind the raw edges with masking tape or fold over a ½-in. selvage to the back and machine-hem to prevent raveling.

When working with as many colors as are in the Alphabet Garden rug, it's essential to organize your materials. Before stitching, separate the yarns according to color families. Label each color with its color number as it appears on the key of the color charts. This will facilitate your stitching and prevent you from misplacing yarns or using the wrong color.

To begin stitching, determine the placement of the design on the hemmed canvas. First, stitch the entire three-stitch-wide black grid across the canvas to establish the 6-in. squares of the design. Note that the J and the Q drop below the grid; leave a space for each letter and fill in the grid after the letter is completed.

Following the alphabet floral charts and referring to the photograph on the facing page for placement, stitch each of the floral letters. Begin with the letter A and work across in horizontal rows, filling every other square with a letter. Fill in the backgrounds with the appropriate colors as indicated in the corner of each chart. (This will leave the last two squares in the lower-right corner of the rug blank for the striated background squares.)

For the alternating background squares, cut the desired yarn colors into random lengths and place them in a bag or basket. Work each square in horizontal or vertical rows as desired using a random, grab-bag selection of colors for a striated effect.

Because of the many colors within the floral letter designs, almost any colors will work for the background grab-bag colors. Purchase a sufficient amount of whatever colors you choose or use up yarn remnants from other projects for a money-saving, scrap-craft effect.

To finish, stitch a 10-stitch-wide border around the outside of the grid using 710 Mustard.

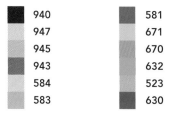

■ 940		■ 581	
947		671	
945		670	
943		632	
584		523	
583		■ 630	

Work the background of each letter in the color indicated in the corner of the chart.

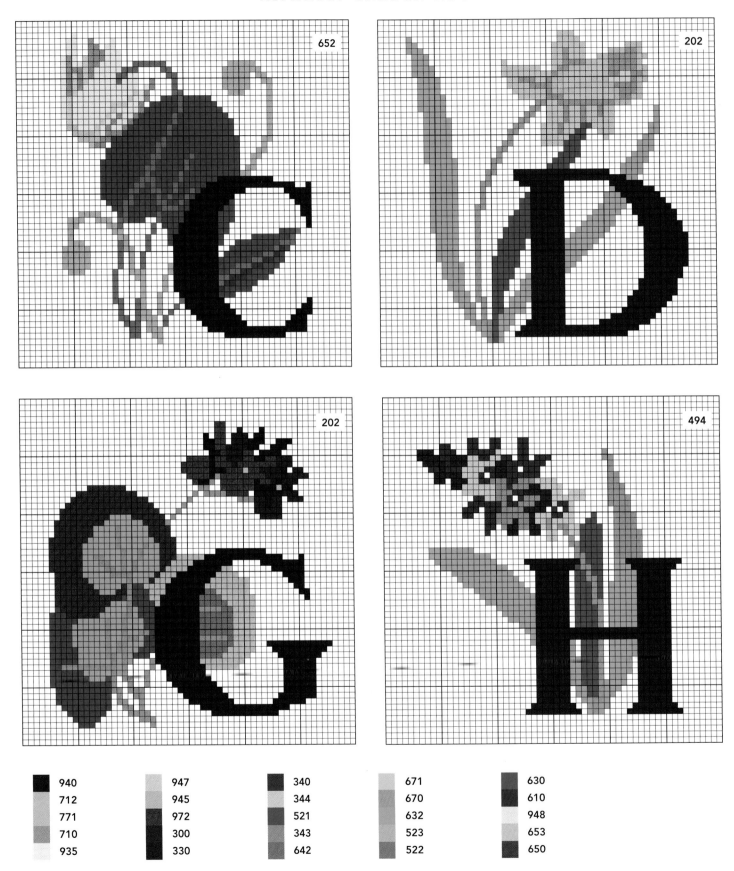

■	940		947		340		671		630
	712		945		344		670		610
	771		972		521		632		948
	710		300		343		523		653
	935		330		642		522		650

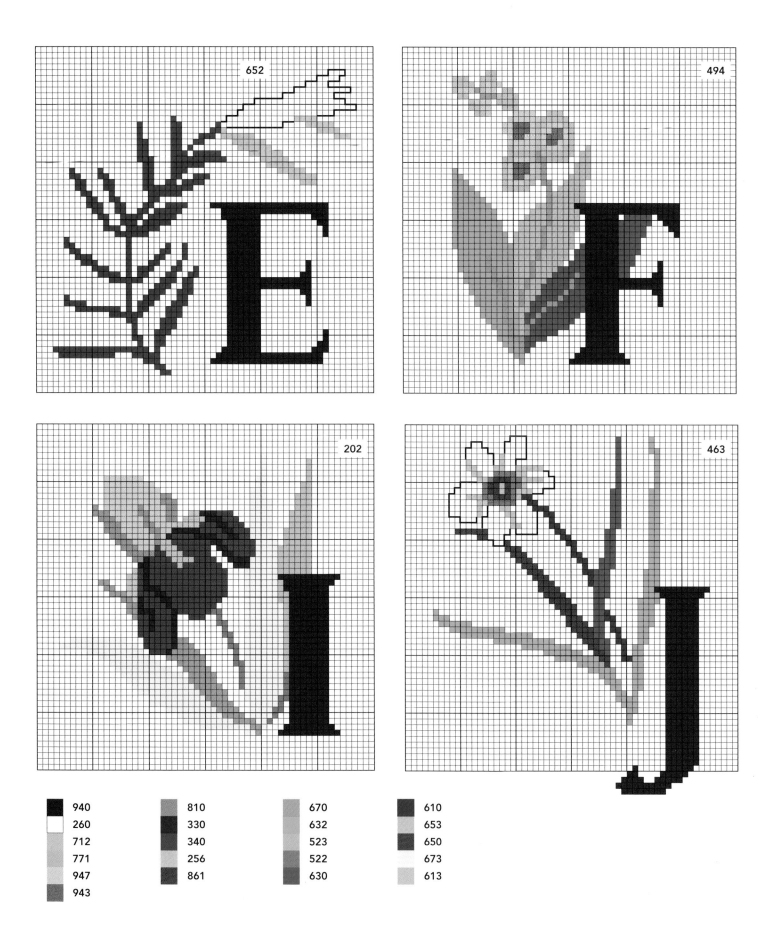

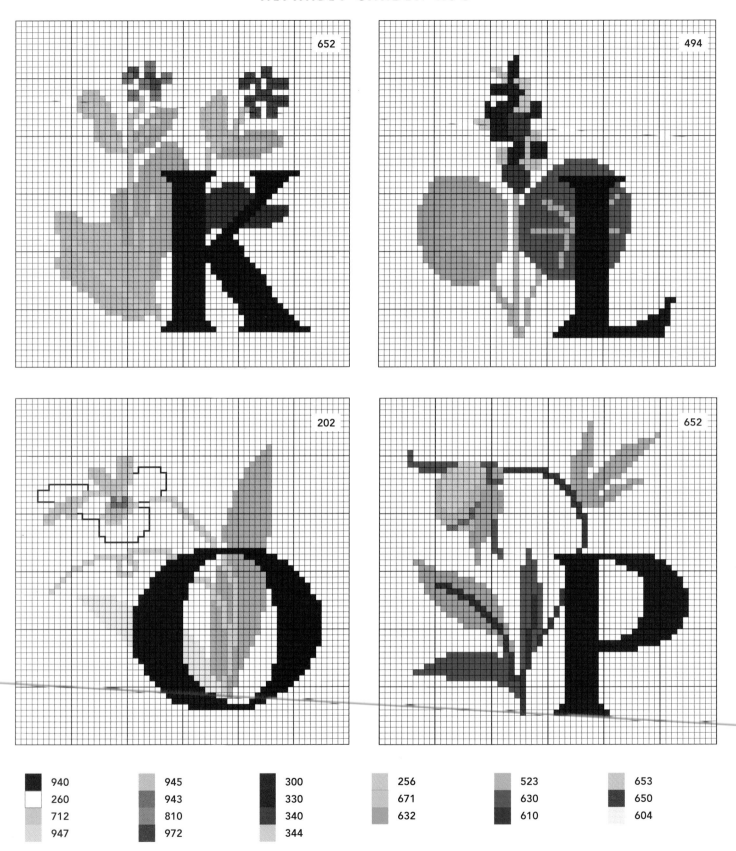

■ 940	▨ 945	■ 300	▨ 256	▨ 523	▨ 653
□ 260	▨ 943	■ 330	▨ 671	■ 630	■ 650
▨ 712	▨ 810	■ 340	▨ 632	■ 610	▨ 604
▨ 947	■ 972	▨ 344			

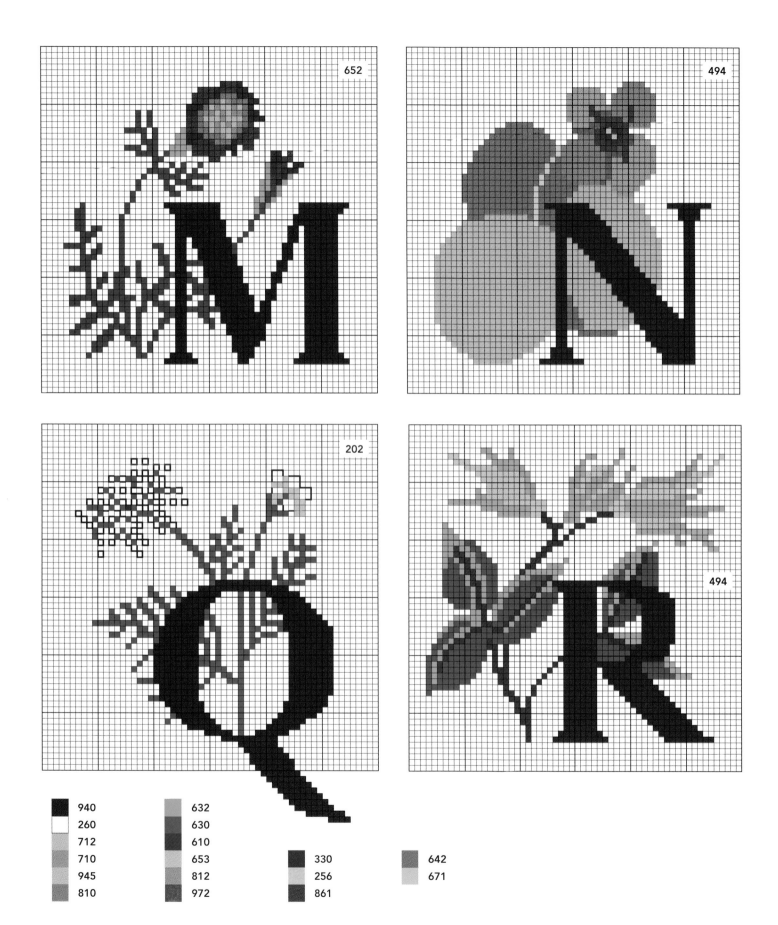

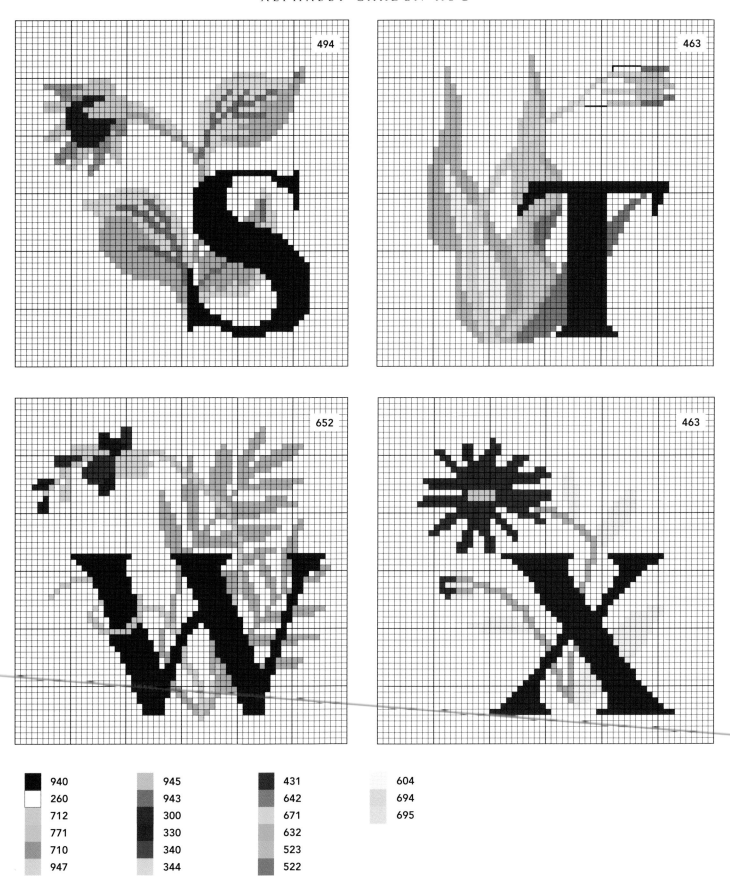

■ 940	945	431	604	
□ 260	943	642	694	
712	300	671	695	
771	330	632		
710	340	523		
947	344	522		

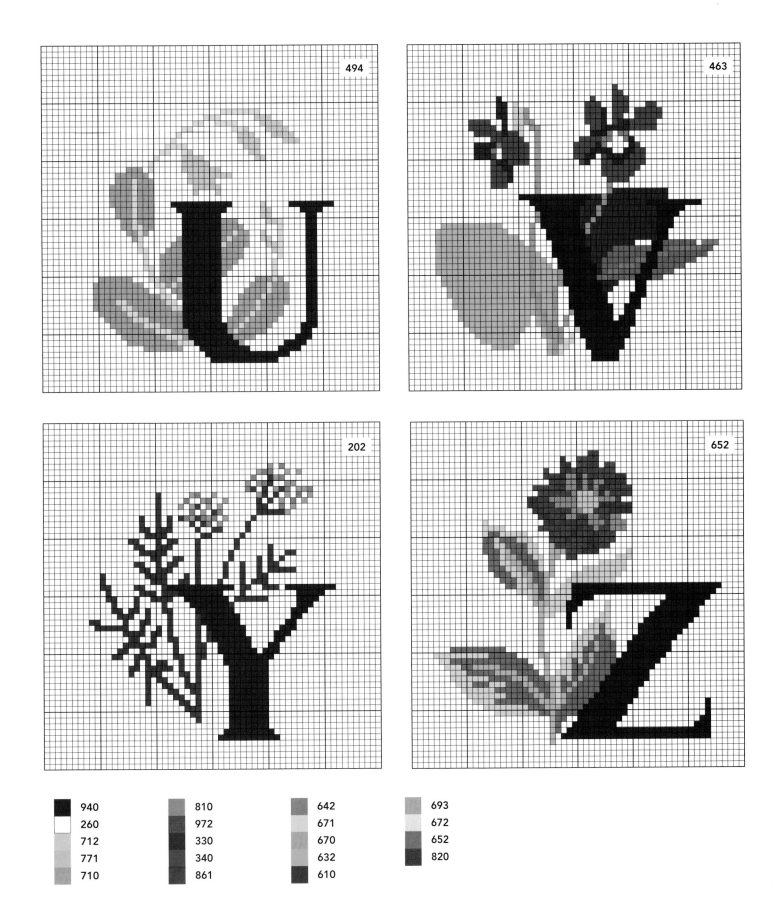

940	810	642	693
260	972	671	672
712	330	670	652
771	340	632	820
710	861	610	

COUNTRY ROSE WREATH

Finished size: approximately 14 in. square

A ring of old-fashioned single-petaled roses creates an everlasting wreath for you to stitch and enjoy. Framed in rustic twigs, it makes a country accent for your wall, but it would be just as appealing as an accent pillow or worked on a finer canvas as a rose-scented sachet.

What You Need

- 18-in. square of #10 mono canvas
- Tapestry needle
- Yarns in the following colors and amounts (all colors are Paternayan 3-ply Persian wool):

For the roses:

350 6 yd.		**824** 3 yd.	
961 6 yd.		**711** 3 yd.	
904 15 yd.		**773** 6 yd.	
954 9 yd.		**445** 6 yd.	
955 12 yd.		**246** 16 yd.	
946 30 yd.		**260** 9 yd.	

For the leaves:

692 12 yd.		**652** 15 yd.	
693 9 yd.			

For the background:

663
180 yd. (one ¼-lb. hank)

Framing Your Needlework

A frame for your stitchery is an attractive and simple alternative to pillows as a form of display, as in the Country Rose Wreath pictured here.

To frame your piece, begin by blocking the needlepoint according to the directions on p. 99.

Select a frame that complements the subject, style, and design of your needlework. The custom-built twig frame suggests the country flavor of the wild roses, but many purchased frames would work as well. It is essential, too, that the frame fit your piece. If not, consider using a colored or fabric-covered mat to make any adjustments and to add a further accent.

Note that the fibers of textiles need to "breathe," so it is advisable not to place your stitching under glass. If you wish to use glass over your stitching, it is best to take your piece to a reputable framing dealer for a professional, museum-quality framing.

To frame your stitchery yourself, cut a piece of cardboard or mat board to fit the needlework. Center the board on the back of the stitchery and, one side at a time, fold the selvages over the board. Hot-glue the selvage in place. Repeat for all sides, working one side and then the opposite side, taking care to stretch but not distort the stitchery across the front of the board.

For the corners, cut the selvage at a 45° angle across the corner near the corner of the stitching, and then glue each folded flap in place.

Place the needlepoint and board into the frame and secure with small wire brads. Back the selvage-covered board with a second piece of cardboard, mat board, or foam core for a finished look, and add a wire for hanging.

What to Do

To prepare the canvas for stitching, bind the raw edges with masking tape or fold over a ½-in. selvage to the back and machine-hem to prevent raveling.

To begin stitching, determine the placement of the design on the canvas. Working with all three plies of yarn, select a rose to start and stitch its center.

Continue working that flower, and then stitch the adjoining bloom. Work all the blossoms in the circle, then stitch the rose buds and leaves. Finish by filling in the background with 663 Pine Green.

COUNTRY ROSE
WREATH

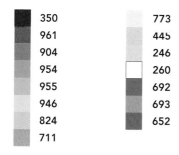

350	773
961	445
904	246
954	260
955	692
946	693
824	652
711	

Work the background in 663.

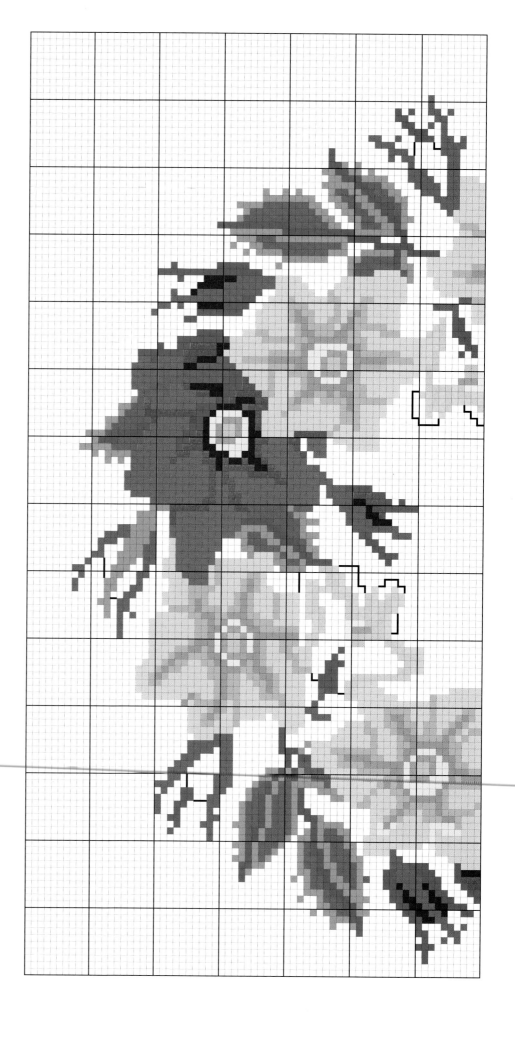

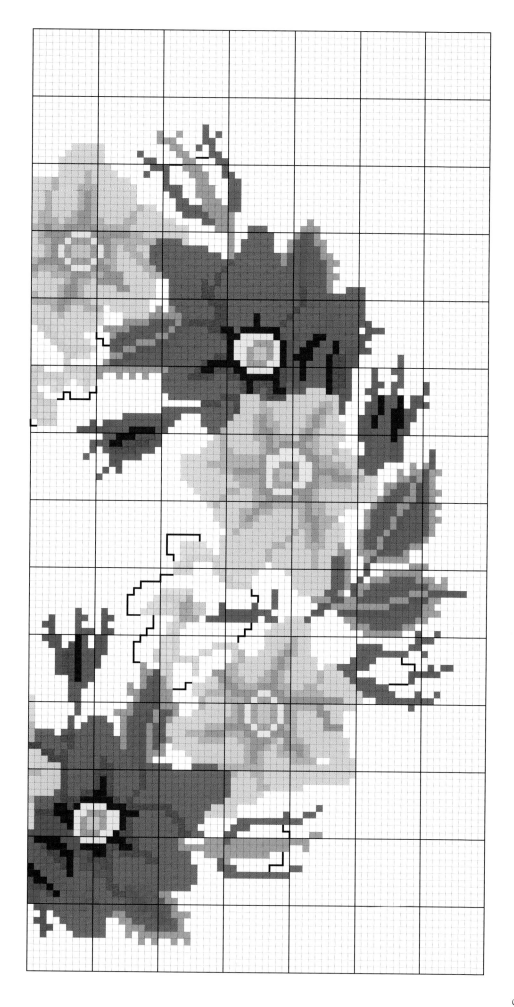

PRIMROSE RUG

Finished size: approximately 36 in. by 52 in.

Old-fashioned primulas are a sure sign of spring as their dainty but colorful blooms reach up to greet us. Crisp black and white checks set off this plot of rainbow-hued primroses and delicate bluebells. The flowers sprouting in the earthy tweed garden are a repeat design that can be worked to any size, with the border added.

What You Need

- 56-in. length of #10 mono canvas
- Tapestry needle
- Fine-point indelible marker
- Yarns in the following colors and amounts (all colors are Paternayan 3-ply Persian wool; yarn amounts are for the 36-in. by 52-in. rug pictured, with the amounts for one repeat of the design given in parentheses):

For the leaves:

670	120 (15) yd.	673	160 (20) yd.
692	48 (6) yd.	612	120 (15) yd.
650	160 (20) yd.	672	160 (20) yd.
693	128 (16) yd.	695	72 (9) yd.

For the primroses:

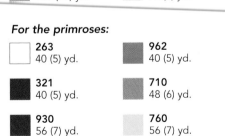

263	40 (5) yd.	962	40 (5) yd.
321	40 (5) yd.	710	48 (6) yd.
930	56 (7) yd.	760	56 (7) yd.

What to Do

To prepare the canvas for stitching, bind the raw edges with masking tape or fold over a ½-in. selvage to the back and machine-hem to prevent raveling.

To begin stitching, determine the placement of the design on the hemmed canvas. To do this, mark a rectangle a few inches in from the hemmed edges with a fine-point indelible marker. (For the 36-in. by 52-in. rug pictured on the facing page, the rectangle should measure 26 in. by 44 in.) This line represents the *outer* edge of the narrow gold border stripe of the design. Note that in order to make the checked border fit evenly all around, it is essential that the drawn rectangle be in increments of whole inches.

For the bluebells:

340	40 (5) yd.	333	64 (8) yd.

For the background:

423	128 yd.	752	64 yd.

For the borders:

263	90 yd.	700	75 yd.
220	154 yd.	520	966 yd.

Using the chart of the repeat design as a reference (see pp. 84-85), determine the placement of the floral pattern. To do this, count the squares on the chart up from the lower-right corner of the marked line to determine the placement of the pink primrose plant. Stitch this plant, and then continue to work the entire floral repeat.

Continue to work the repeats across the entire marked rectangle, fitting each repeat into the former as indicated on the chart. As you reach the edge of the marked rectangle, stitch any primrose plant in its entirety beyond the line; omit any bluebells.

Stitch the four-stitch-wide gold border all around with 700 Butterscotch between the overlapping plants following the marked line.

Fill in the background "soil" with two plies of 423 Coffee Brown and one ply of 752 Old Gold.

Beginning in the upper-right corner of the gold border strip, stitch a 1-in. square (10 stitches by 10 stitches) using 263 White. Alternate black and white checks all around and between any overlapping plants.

To finish, using the photograph as a guide, position and stitch the alphabet (see pp. 86-87) along the lower border of the rug in 220 Black or any color desired. (Portions of the alphabet may fall under overlapping plants.) Fill in the border with 520 Dark Teal.

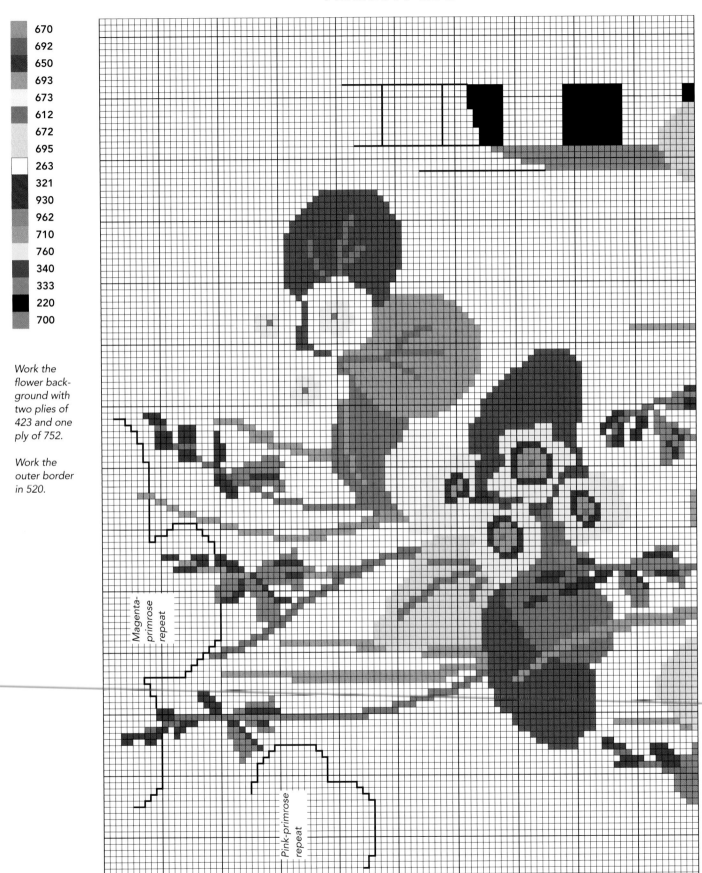

670
692
650
693
673
612
672
695
263
321
930
962
710
760
340
333
220
700

Work the flower background with two plies of 423 and one ply of 752.

Work the outer border in 520.

Magenta-primrose repeat

Pink-primrose repeat

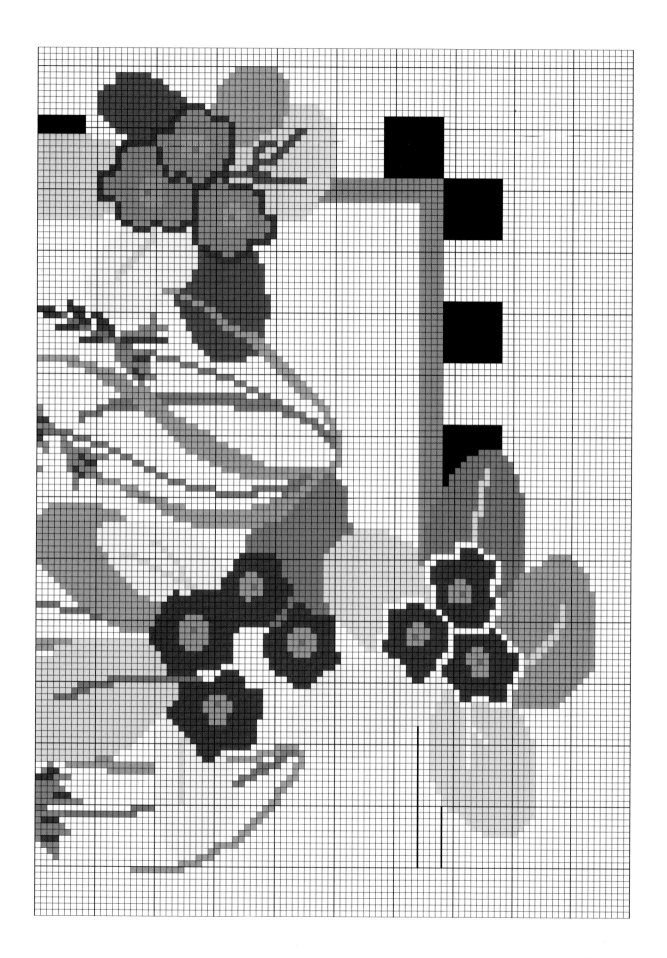

Blending Yarns and Changing Dye Lots

As hard as you try to purchase the correct amount of yarn for a project, there are times when you are faced with running out of a particular color and having to purchase more—oftentimes in a different dye lot or shade altogether.

I personally have no difficulty with changing yarns if necessary. I find that a subtle difference can add a touch of personality, spontaneity, and humanity to the piece. Remember that, in Amish culture, it was felt that only God could make things perfectly, so changes were accepted and "mistakes" were often deliberately sewn into their beautiful quilts.

If the areas you are working on are separate, you can simply substitute the new yarn in place of the old, and no one will be any the wiser. If, as in the case of the teal border for the Primrose Rug, the area is large and continuous, the difference may be more noticeable.

To make the switch in yarns more subtle, try blending the yarns together. When you realize that you do not have enough yarn to complete the area, stop stitching before you run out. Save several strands to use in blending. Take these to your local yarn shop to match the new yarn as closely as possible.

To blend the new color into the old, no matter how close they match, begin working with two plies of the old color and one ply of the new for at least 1 in. Then work with two plies of the new and one ply of the old. Finally, begin stitching in three plies of the new yarn to finish the area.

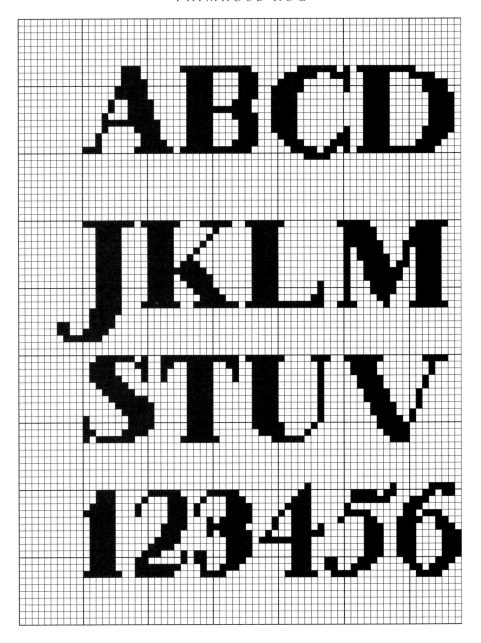

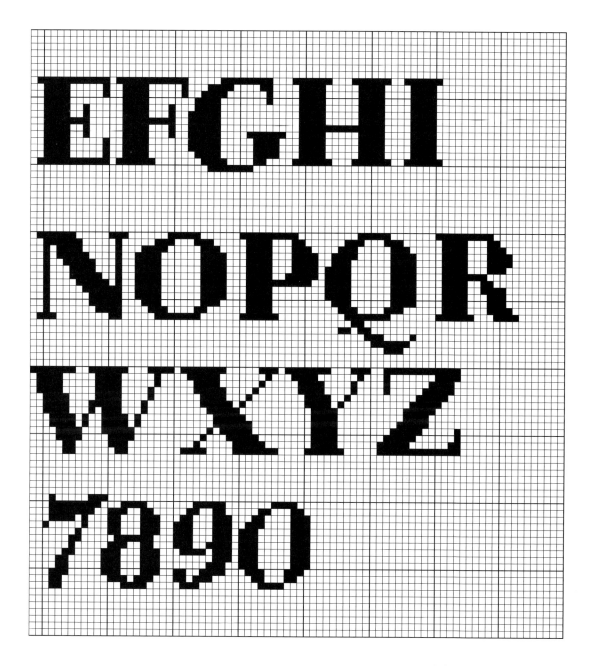

Work the alphabet in 220 Black or color desired.

PANSY BLANKET BORDER

Finished size: one repeat of three flowers, approximately 12 in.

*B*right *pansies blooming all in a row create a garden-fresh border for a country wool throw that echoes their colors. Work the blossoms as many times as needed to match the width of the blanket.*

What You Need

- 9-in.-wide piece of #10 mono canvas in desired length
- Tapestry needle
- Yarns in the following colors and amounts (all colors are Paternayan 3-ply Persian wool; yarn amounts are for one repeat):

For the pansies:

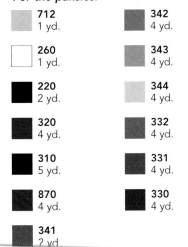

712 1 yd.		342 4 yd.	
260 1 yd.		343 4 yd.	
220 2 yd.		344 4 yd.	
320 4 yd.		332 4 yd.	
310 5 yd.		331 4 yd.	
870 4 yd.		330 4 yd.	
341 2 yd.			

What to Do

To prepare the canvas for stitching, bind the raw edges with masking tape or fold over a ½-in. selvage to the back and machine-hem to prevent raveling.

To begin stitching, determine the placement of the design on the canvas (see the chart on pp. 90-91). Stitch the center of the first pansy, and then finish the flower. Work the other two flowers of the repeat, and then stitch the leaves.

To continue the design, work the first pansy next to the right-hand leaves a second time. Continue the three-flower repeat until the entire length is covered.

Depending on the desired length, the flowers can be stopped at any point—simply omit any charted leaves to the right of the last stitched flower and mark off about 1 in. to the right of the last flower for the background. To finish, work the background of the strip in 263 White.

Assemble the blanket according to the instructions in the sidebar below.

For the leaves:

693 5 yd.		652 5 yd.	
631 5 yd.		650 2 yd.	
692 2 yd.		690 6 yd.	

For the background:

263 60 yd.	

For finishing:

- Medium-weight wool blanket or yardage of fabric in desired size
- 1 yd. to 2 yd. of coordinating linen fabric for cording and needlepoint backing
- ¼-in. cording in length to fit around needlepoint

Blanket Assembly

Block the strip and attach the cording and fabric backing according to the directions on pp. 99-103. Leave the bottom edge of the strip open.

Note that if you are using wool fabric instead of a purchased blanket, bind the edges of the wool with a blanket stitch or use two layers and sew with right sides together. Turn and press, and then proceed.

Insert the fabric or blanket into the opening in the strip and pin securely. Machine-stitch the front of the needlepoint strip to the blanket. Steam-press to flatten the strip if necessary.

To finish, fold under the raw edge of the fabric backing and blind-stitch it to the back of the blanket.

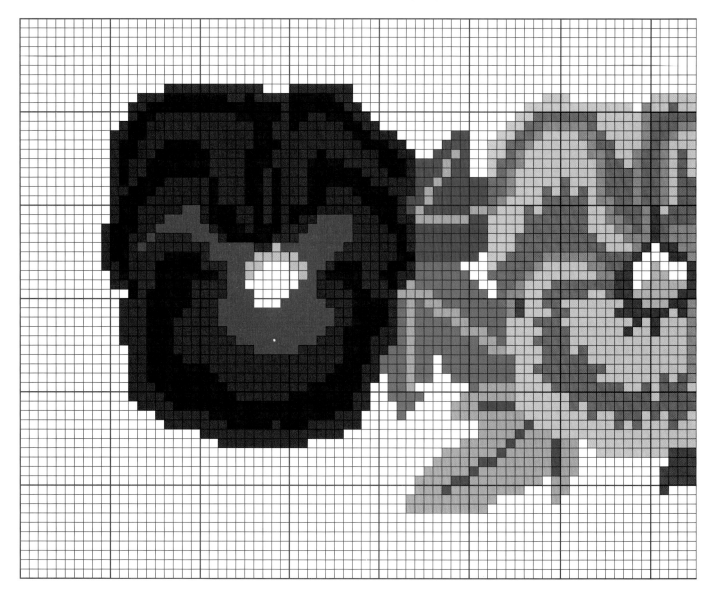

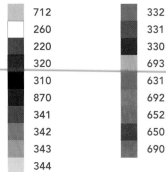

712	332	
260	331	
220	330	
320	693	
310	631	
870	692	
341	652	
342	650	
343	690	
344		

Work the background in 263.

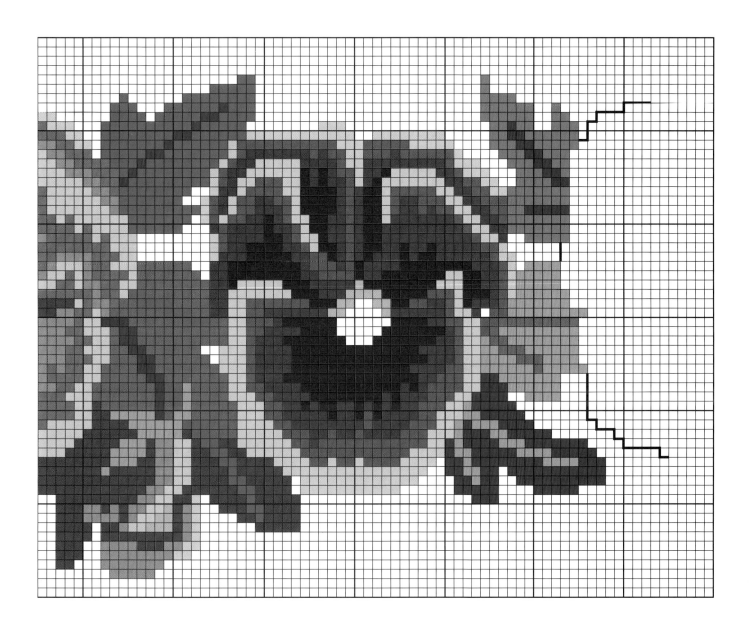

MULTIFLOWER BOUQUET RUG

Finished size: approximately 29 in. by 41 in.

Pluck summer's colors from the garden and bunch them in bouquets of vivid sunflowers, coneflowers, zinnias, and nasturtiums for this extraordinary pieced needlepoint and crocheted rag rug. Stitch the three bouquet panels, then crochet squares from cotton strips in coordinating colors as accents.

What You Need

- Three 15-in. squares of #10 mono canvas
- Tapestry needle
- Yarns in the following colors and amounts (all colors are Paternayan 3-ply Persian wool unless otherwise noted):

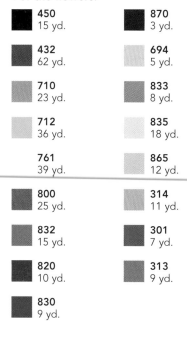

For the flowers:

450 15 yd.		870 3 yd.	
432 62 yd.		694 5 yd.	
710 23 yd.		833 8 yd.	
712 36 yd.		835 18 yd.	
761 39 yd.		865 12 yd.	
800 25 yd.		314 11 yd.	
832 15 yd.		301 7 yd.	
820 10 yd.		313 9 yd.	
830 9 yd.			

DMC embroidery floss

400 3 skeins		444 3 skeins	

What to Do

To prepare the canvases for stitching, bind the raw edges with masking tape or fold over a ½-in. selvage to the back and machine-hem to prevent raveling.

To begin stitching, determine the placement of the first design on the hemmed canvas. Work the center of the large sunflower, and then stitch the petals around it. Continue to work the design following the chart on p. 95. Finish the square by filling in the background. For added detail in the sunflower centers, work the grid couching and star flowers following the diagrams on p. 65 using embroidery flosses 400 and 444. Work the remaining two squares in the same manner, following the charts on pp. 96–97.

For the leaves:

670 3 yd.		693 14 yd.	
652 45 yd.		692 36 yd.	
651 37 yd.		691 13 yd.	

For the background:

403 540 yd. (three ¼-lb. skeins)	

For the crocheted squares:

- 8 yd. to 10 yd. of coordinating cotton fabrics
- Size 11 crochet hook

For finishing:

- Quilt batting or fusible fleece
- Three 13-in. squares of coordinating wool or felt for backing
- Carpet thread
- Sharp tapestry needle
- Hot-glue gun and glue

To prepare the squares for assembling into the rug, block each piece according to the instructions on p. 99. Trim the selvage to ¾ in. all around. Cut off each corner at a 45° angle close to the stitched corner to allow the selvage to lie flat. Fold over the selvage to the back and hot-glue in place.

Cut batting or fusible fleece to fit each square. Place the fleece atop the back of the stitching, and then cover with the backing fabric. Fold under the raw edges of the fabric and whipstitch it to the edges of the needlepoint stitching with carpet thread. Set aside.

Crochet three squares following the instructions in the sidebar on p. 94.

To assemble the rug, arrange the squares in the desired order referring to the photo for placement. Using carpet thread, stitch a crocheted square to a needlepoint square, adjusting the stitching of the crocheted piece as necessary to fit. Repeat for the other two pairs of panels, then stitch the pairs together to create the six-panel rug.

For the border, attach a fabric strip to one corner of a crocheted square. Single crochet (sc) along the edge until you reach the needlepoint square. Chain (ch) the strip to fit the length of the needlepoint. Sew the chain to the edge of the needlepoint stitching, adjusting as necessary to fit, and then sc along the edge of the next crocheted square. Continue all around the rug.

Double crochet (dc) 3 times into the first stitch of the former row to make the corner. Sc along the crocheted and chained row to the corner. Dc 3 times into the corner stitch to make a square corner, then sc to the next corner. Dc 3 times in the corner stitch. Repeat for five rows or desired width.

Making a Crocheted Square

To prepare the fabric for crocheting, cut each piece into 1-in.-wide strips. For the random coloration of the squares pictured in the Multiflower Bouquet Rug, machine- or hand-sew the strips together in random, grab-bag fashion. Roll the strips into balls to store.

To begin the square, tie the end of the strip loosely around the crochet hook. **Row 1:** Ch 4, then put hook through original knot. **Row 2:** Sc 6 around circle. Put hook through first sc to begin next row. **Row 3:** To make square shape, sc 1, dc 3 in next stitch, sc 1, dc 3 in next stitch, sc 1, dc 3 in next stitch, sc 1, dc 3 in next stitch. **Rows 4 and consecutive rows:** Sc around, with dc 3 times in corner stitches to make corners. Repeat rows until the crocheted square is the same size as the needlepoint squares (about 10 rows).

CHAIN STITCH (CH)

1. Insert hook into slip knot, wrap yarn over, and pull yarn through to form chain.

2. Repeat to form number of chains required.

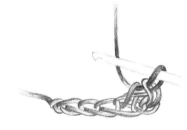

SINGLE CROCHET (SC)

1. Insert hook into second chain from hook, wrap yarn over, and pull yarn through work.

2. Yarn over again and pull through two loops on hook.

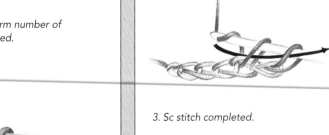

3. Sc stitch completed.

DOUBLE CROCHET (DC)

1. Wrap yarn over and insert hook into fourth chain.

2. Yarn over again and pull through work.

3. Yarn over and pull through first two loops.

4. Yarn over and pull through last two loops on hook.

5. Dc stitch completed.

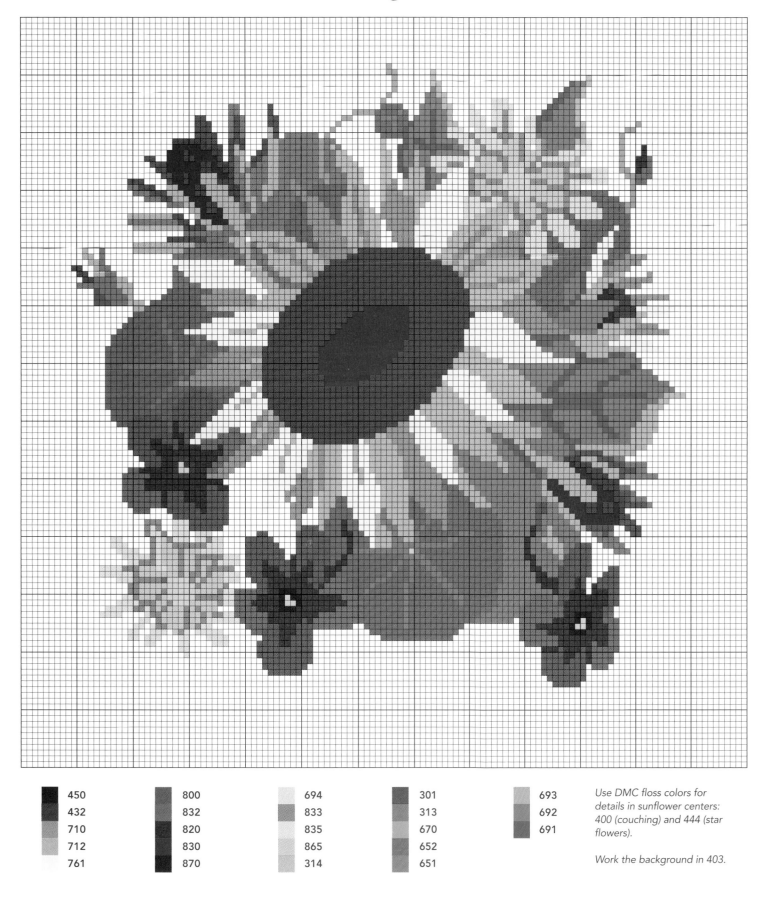

	450		800		694		301		693
	432		832		833		313		692
	710		820		835		670		691
	712		830		865		652		
	761		870		314		651		

Use DMC floss colors for details in sunflower centers: 400 (couching) and 444 (star flowers).

Work the background in 403.

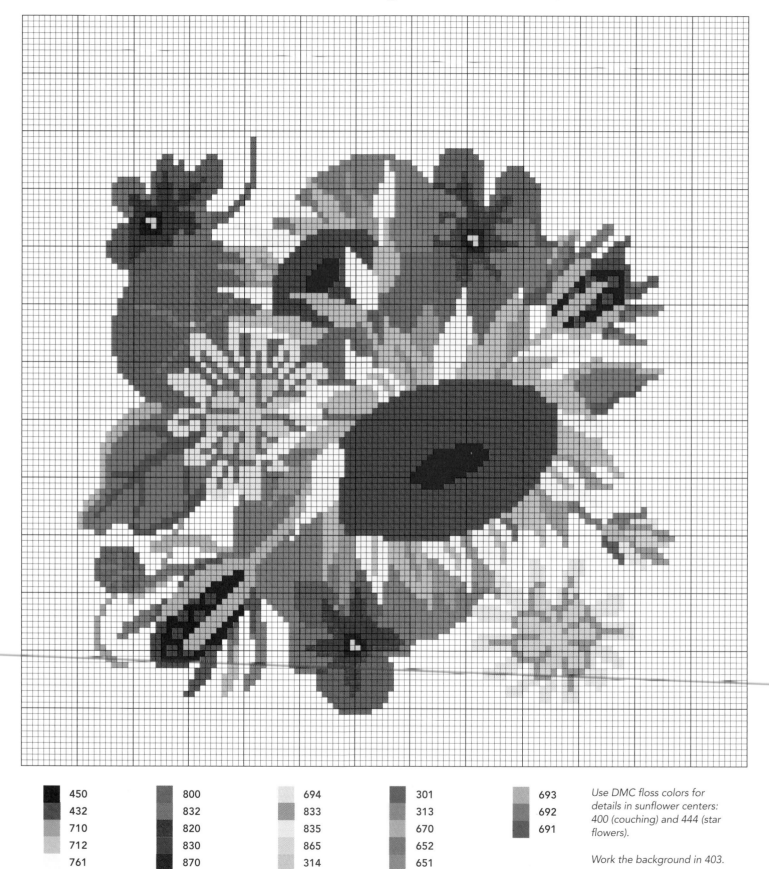

450	800	694	301	693	Use DMC floss colors for details in sunflower centers: 400 (couching) and 444 (star flowers).
432	832	833	313	692	
710	820	835	670	691	
712	830	865	652		Work the background in 403.
761	870	314	651		

450	800	694	301	693
432	832	833	313	692
710	820	835	670	691
712	830	865	652	
761	870	314	651	

Use DMC floss colors for details in sunflower centers: 400 (couching) and 444 (star flowers).

Work the background in 403.

FINISHING TIPS AND TECHNIQUES

Needlepoint is a rewarding pastime, but it can be a costly and time-consuming endeavor, particularly when stitching large projects. Proper finishing and selection of fabrics for your needlework will allow you to make the most of your labor of love—and give your stitchery a professional look, a personality, and a lasting heirloom quality.

Blocking Your Needlepoint

Blocking your finished piece is essential to a professional presentation. Many times during stitching the canvas will distort because of the stitcher's individual tension while working. Blocking returns the canvas to its original shape and helps to smooth out any uneven stitches.

For best results when blocking, mist the finished needlepoint lightly with cool water. Don't soak the canvas to block it. Dyes used in the yarns, especially those in untraditional fibers, may bleed and ruin your work. Staple your stitchery to a fabric-covered blocking board cut from ¼-in. plywood. The board should be 2 in. larger all around than the needlework. Prolific stitchers may wish to make one board large enough to fit a rug and use it for several smaller projects as well. Cover the board with fabric to prevent any stains from the wood from discoloring your stitching. I prefer to cover my blocking boards with an inexpensive white or natural flannel—I find that the softness gives added protection to the needlepoint stitching.

Begin by stapling along one edge of the canvas with a staple gun, aligning the selvage parallel to the edge of the board. Next, pulling the canvas taut and square as you go, staple every 2 in. to 3 in. around the canvas. Mist again with water as necessary, and allow the piece to dry flat on the board.

Once the needlepoint has dried, remove the canvas from the board. To do this, use a screwdriver to pry up one end of each staple and pull them out with a pair of pliers. If the needlework is not yet square, remist the piece and repeat the blocking process. I find that it's necessary to reblock when a piece has been badly warped due to the tension of the stitch or a directional stitch. (To minimize this problem, don't pull the yarn when stitching—simply lay it upon the canvas, and work directional stitches across and then back across the canvas.)

When the needlepoint is blocked to your satisfaction, you can proceed to finish your work. In preparation, trim the hemmed selvage to about 1 in. from the edge of the stitching all around.

Finishing Rugs

For rugs, there are several finishing options to consider. You may wish simply to turn the selvage under and fold back and whipstitch it to the back of the needlepoint stitching. You might also consider stitching purchased bias tape to the raw canvas, and then folding the selvage back and sewing (see the photo above). Either way will provide a neat hem for your rug. For best results, be sure to turn about three needlepoint stitches under so that no raw canvas shows from the front.

Another option is to stitch a length of fabric-covered cording around the edge of the rug, much as you would around a pillow (see p. 102), and then turn back the selvage and sew it to the back of the needlepoint stitching. The cording will provide a finished edge that frames the stitchery, much like the cording that defines the needlepoint and braiding of the Cock Crows at Dawn Rug (see p. 23).

Backing your hemmed rug with fabric provides a professional finish. The fabric covers the unsightly back of the stitching and also aids in preventing threads from coming loose and

stitches from unraveling. To back your rug with fabric, cut a length of inexpensive cotton fabric about 1 in. larger than your rug all around, piecing if necessary. With right sides together, fold under the raw edges of the fabric and hand-sew it all around to the folded edge of the stitching with carpet thread.

It is perfectly acceptable not to back your rug if you so choose; just clip any threads that remain hanging from the back of the stitchery. Although this is not the neatest presentation, it does make it simpler to clean and to reblock if necessary should the canvas go out of shape.

Selecting Fabric

The fabrics that you choose for pillows can greatly enhance your needlepoint stitchery. I prefer to do a lot of mixing and matching of fabrics because I feel that it gives each piece a unique quality and a personality that cannot be found in store-bought pillows. Furthermore, the fabric selection and treatment become a creative extension of the needlepoint itself.

I look for unusual fabrics, such as upholstery or drapery fabrics, vintage remnants from antiques shops and flea markets, old jeans, cut-out areas of worn and tattered blankets and quilts, wool suiting, or even dress fabrics to use in my pillows. The Southwestern Hen pillow on p. 19 is framed with a remnant of a worn and weathered Indian blanket. The Rooster pillow on p. 7 is bordered with a wonderfully textured raw-silk dress or suit fabric from a dressmaker's shop, and the Indian Corn pillow's ruffle on p. 57 is fashioned from an entire vintage dish towel—the center of the towel was cut out for the pillow and the outside edges gathered to fit. Use your imagination when it comes to deciding upon the fabrics you can employ.

Color is perhaps the most important consideration when selecting your fabrics. The fabrics should coordinate with the colors in the needlepoint and not detract from what they are to frame. For the vibrant Zinnia pillow at right, a simple coordinating velvet encircles the piece and does not compete with the multicolored stitching.

For less complicated pieces, think about using a combination of stripes, a small check, and a contrasting solid, as in the Rabbits in Clover pillow on p. 27. The brown of the stripe matches the tweed "earth" background, while the pink/brown bias mini-check picks up the colors of the rabbits and clover. The solid magenta cording acts as a framing contrast that accents the clover.

The Cabbage and Caterpillar pillow on p. 49 is another example of the fabrics' showing off the needlepoint. The stripe of the pleated ruffle echoes the subtle coloration within the cabbage, while the vintage upholstery fabric on the cording both accents and contrasts with the stitching.

Finishing Details

Finishing details give your work a professional look. I feel that piping, cording, and ruffles are extra touches that really make your stitching stand out. With a little practice, you can use any or all of these elements to finish your work.

Piping is a narrow cord that can be purchased in a number of standard shades. It is also available braided or woven in a variety of colors. The Poppy pillow on p. 59 uses black commercial braided piping around the raw canvas of the poppy design. You can make your own fabric piping if the color you

have in mind is not available. Cording is a larger version of piping, and most often comes as an inexpensive white cotton cord that you cover yourself.

To make your own piping or cording, determine the length and size of cord you will need for your project. Cut the desired fabric into strips to cover the cord with about 1 in. selvage on each side. For best effect, cut your strips on the bias, which allows for greater flexibility and give, especially on round pieces. It is sometimes beneficial, however, to cut the strips with the grain, particularly on checks and stripes, which lend themselves to a vertical format. Piece your strips together if necessary by mitering each end to a 45° angle. For straight-grained strips, piece at 90°.

To sew the fabric to the cord, use the zipper-foot attachment of your machine and stitch along the covered strip near to the cord. For the large cording that appears on the Rooster pillow on p. 7 and the Farm Cat on p. 37, it's best to gather the fabric slightly on the cord because it is difficult to have the fabric lie flat when assembling.

Ruffles, too, can do a lot to individualize and accent your stitchery. If you opt for a ruffled edging, there are many possibilities to choose from. Make sure, however, that the ruffle is ample—2 in. to 3 in. wide and two to two-and-a-half times the perimeter of the pillow. For example, if the pillow is 12 in. square, the ruffle should be at least 8 ft. long.

Ruffles may be cut on the bias or on the straight grain, and they can be as simple as a double width of fabric folded over and gathered. If you're using a heavier-weight fabric, use a single layer and piece together with flat-felled seams if necessary.

For a different look, consider edging the ruffle with a bias strip of fabric, as in the Rabbits in Clover pillow on p. 27, or fringe a length of linen for a rustic, country ruffle, as in the Concord Grapes pillow on the facing page or the Poppy pillow on p. 59. To fringe the ruffle, stitch a line with matching thread ¾ in. to 1 in. from one end of a single layer of linen. Piece linen if necessary with flat-felled seams, and then unravel the fabric's threads to the sewn line.

Other options include adding a narrow lace or tatted edging or sewing a length of commercial rickrack into the edge of the ruffle. Whatever you choose, practice a degree of restraint. Don't use too many different options on one pillow. Fewer choices executed well will make more of a statement than several techniques competing against each other.

To gather the fabric into a ruffle, use a gathering stitch on your machine or a zigzag stitch over a piece of string about ½ in. from the raw edges. Pull the gathering threads or string until the ruffle is the desired fullness.

Folding the strip into a pleated ruffle is another possibility, as in the Cabbage pillow on p. 49. To pleat the ruffle, fold and pin the fabric strip into 2-in. pleats. Secure by stitching a line about ½ in. from the raw edge.

Assembling Pillows

Once you've stitched the cording and/or the ruffle and chosen your backing fabric, you are ready to assemble your needlepoint pillow.

Beginning at the bottom center of the pillow, and with the needlepoint right side up, pin the cording to the selvage of the needlepoint. Position the cord atop the needlepoint stitching with the selvage over the canvas. Pin all around, and then trim away any excess cording, leaving at least 1 in. of fabric selvage on the cording. Place the cording selvage over the starting end of the cord, folding in the raw edge of the cording strip. Sew the cording in place using the zipper-foot attachment of your machine, and then hand-stitch the folded edge to the cording to secure.

Next, pin and stitch the ruffle atop the cording in the same manner as for the cording, with the *outer* edge of the ruffle atop the needlepoint and the raw edge aligning with the raw edges of the cord and canvas. If the ruffle is a two-layer fold, tuck one end into the other, fold under the raw edges of the top ruffle, and hand-stitch together.

If the ruffle is a single layer, join the ruffle with a flat-felled seam, and then adjust the gathers all around the pillow, pin, and sew.

Cut your backing fabric to size, adding about a 1-in. selvage all around. For a smoother surface, line the backing with fleece, especially if you are using a lightweight fabric.

With right sides together, sew around the pillow atop the previous stitch lines and as close to the cording as possible, leaving an opening for turning. Trim the fabrics and canvas, clipping any curves. Turn the pillow to its right side and press the ruffle if necessary.

To stuff the pillow, I find that it's best to create your own pillow form from muslin and polyester fiberfill. For a firm, smooth pillow, make a pillow form at least 2 in. larger than the finished pillow. Stitch the muslin pieces together, leaving an opening for turning and stuffing. Turn, stuff, and sew the opening closed.

To make the pillow corners fuller, pack a small amount of fiberfill into each corner before stuffing. Insert the custom form into your pillow, taking care to pack it firmly. Sew the opening closed.

PUBLISHER
Suzanne La Rosa

ACQUISITIONS EDITOR
Jolynn Gower

PUBLISHING COORDINATOR
Sarah Coe

EDITOR
Peter Chapman

DESIGNER/LAYOUT ARTIST
Carol Singer

ILLUSTRATOR
Rosalie Vaccaro

PHOTOGRAPHERS
Boyd Hagen (pgs. 44, 83)
Scott Phillips (pgs. viii, 4, 5, 98, 100, 102)
John Ryman (all other photos)

PRODUCTION MANAGER
Lynne Phillips

TYPEFACE
Palatino

PAPER
80-lb. Warren Patina Matte

PRINTER
R.R. Donnelley, Willard, Ohio